BEING
CHRISTIAN
IN AN ALMOST
CHOSEN
NATION

THINKING ABOUT
FAITH AND POLITICS

H. STEPHEN SHOEMAKER

Abingdon Press
Nashville

BEING CHRISTIAN IN AN ALMOST CHOSEN NATION
THINKING ABOUT FAITH AND POLITICS

Library of Congress Cataloging-in-Publication Data

Shoemaker, H. Stephen, 1948-
  Being Christian in an almost chosen nation : thinking about faith and politics / H. Stephen Shoemaker.
     p. cm.
  ISBN 0-687-33423-3 (binding: pbk. adhesive, perfect : alk. paper)
  1. Christianity and politics--United States. 2. Christianity and politics--Baptists. I. Title.
  BR526.S574 2006
  261.70973--dc22

                                                                    2006021138

06 07 08 09 10 11 12 13 14 15—10 9 8 7 6 5 4 3 2 1

MANUFACTURED IN THE UNITED STATES OF AMERICA

I shall be most happy indeed if I shall be an humble instrument
in the hands of the Almighty, and of this his almost chosen people,
for perpetuating the object of that great struggle.
   —Abraham Lincoln
      Address to the New Jersey Senate, February 21, 1861

The ceremony of innocence is drowned;
The best lack all conviction, while the worst
Are full of passionate intensity.
   —W. B. Yeats
      "The Second Coming"

Man is neither angel nor beast; and the misfortune
is that he who would act the angel acts the beast.
   —Blaise Pascal
      Pensées

And now we are stirring up the question whether or not Islam is a
warlike religion, ignoring the question, much more urgent for us,
whether or not Christianity is a warlike religion. There is no hope in
this. Islam, Judaism, Christianity—all have been warlike religions.
   —Wendell Berry
      Citizenship Papers

TO MY TEACHERS

at
Stetson University,
Union Theological Seminary,
New York City,
and
The Southern Baptist Theological Seminary,
Louisville, Kentucky

CONTENTS

Contents

PREFACE

*Horatio: If thou art privy to thy nation's fate, which,
happily, foreknowing may avoid, O speak!*
—*Hamlet*, Act One, Scene 1

Being Christian in an almost chosen nation; thinking about faith and politics in an incendiary age. These phrases speak to the issues and challenges of this book. It probes Christian identity and national identity; how to be a person of specifically Christian faith; how to negotiate the volatile mix of faith and politics in an age where religion seems to be an accelerant on the fires of global politics. How does one try to be a Christian in America in days such as these?

Thomas Merton once wrote that in bad times an ethic of love turns into an ethic of resistance. I find myself in some sad and fierce, sometimes fitful, resistance to the direction I see my nation headed: our nation of idealism and generosity becoming a nation that is a law unto itself, a warrior nation, and a greedy nation whose highest good seems to be economic growth and having "more." I should add: and a wounded nation that found itself savagely attacked by a terrorist fury it only barely comprehended.

The Christian minister is the bearer of two sacred scriptures, Hebrew and Christian. Eminent historian Jaroslav Pelikan has said that the most important decision of the second-century church was to be a people of two books, not just one; that is, of the Hebrew scriptures along with the Christian New Testament. Billy Graham, whose evangelistic work has been a wonder and a great gift to the world, once said that he was called to be a New Testament evangelist, not an Old Testament prophet. It is a distinction Jesus never made, but it does speak to a priority which he maintained and which I myself try to maintain. There are times, however, when the Old Testament prophet part of Jesus comes to the fore.

The biblical prophet, says Paul D. Hanson, is one who applies his or her vision of God and God's will to the realm of "plain history, real politics and human instrumentality."[1] One cannot be a "true prophet" without running the considerable risk of being a "false prophet," that is, being wrong in one's judgments. This is a fearsome prospect. Poet William Stafford wrote of those who decline "to be willingly fallible in order to find their way."[2] The willingness to be fallible is not the way of the world, but it is the beginning of wisdom. Just the beginning.

In his analysis of the current state of the news media, Judge Richard Posner writes that "the public's interest in factual accuracy is less an interest in truth than a delight in the unmasking of the opposition's errors."[3] There is a profound spiritual difference between "wanting to be right" and "wanting to be truthful." I, as anyone, want to be right, but I hope I want more to be truthful, that is faithful to the best truth I can now know and faithful to reality itself. Where I inevitably fail, forgive the errors. They are made in the pursuit of truth and in the faith that there is a truth that corresponds to reality and to the mind of God, however dimly we perceive it.

I write as a Christian minister with his own way of interpreting the biblical traditions in which he has been raised. I have been inordinately blessed with a wide array of extraordinary teachers, in school and out of school. This book is dedicated "to my teachers," of Stetson University, Union Theological Seminary, New York City, and The Southern Baptist Theological Seminary in Louisville, Kentucky.

I here also acknowledge with deep thanks those who helped prepare my final manuscript, Cheryl Collins Patterson, Pat Hice, Velma Stevens, and Amy Jones; two who read my manuscript with careful advice, Russell Crandall and Jack Perry; and especially my editor at Abingdon, Robert Ratcliff, who, reading some of my work, urged me to write this book.

INTRODUCTION

Tasting Ashes in a Land of Falling Towers

A friend in my congregation came back from New York City soon after 9/11. He talked about walking around the devastated site of Ground Zero. A fine, almost invisible dust coated his face and, when he parted his mouth, his tongue. He realized with a kind of sacred awe that what he tasted was not just the dust of fallen towers but mixed there the final dust of those almost three thousand persons whose lives had ended there, their bodies, their blood now ashes so fine they could not be seen, only tasted. "It felt like Communion," my friend said, he an ex-Catholic with a genuflection in his voice, something holy there amid the horror.

Could these ashes become a sacrament of understanding, a mystery made more intelligible as we ponder this new era revealed on that terrible day? A deeper awareness, a more demanding intelligence, a truer empathy, a more encompassing politics is now required of us who walk in a time of falling towers.

We are entering a new era in history at the turn of the twenty-first century. What are the signposts of this new era? Here are six:

One: An America seeking to define its "mission" in a world where it is the world's singular superpower.

Two: A world where religion, once banished to the edge of things in the modern era, has come rushing to the center of things in fundamentalist politics and politicized fundamentalism.

The attempts of Christian, Jewish, and Muslim fundamentalisms to "resacralize" society bring along with their moral passion looming dangers. Karen Armstrong, in her book *The Battle for God: A History of Fundamentalism*, writes, "The hideous September attack shows that when people begin to justify hatred and killing, and thus abandon the compassionate ethic of all the great world religions, they have embarked on a course that represents a defeat of faith."[1]

Three: A world where religious pluralism is a new fact of life—there are more Muslims than Presbyterians now in the United States. Along with this pluralism is the urgent need for inter-faith understanding. As Hans Küng put it: "Peace among the religions is the prerequisite for peace among the nations."[2]

Four: A time of ferment in the consideration of the relationship of moral/spiritual values and the public sphere—what has been termed in the American experience "the separation of church and state."

Five: The deep cultural and political divide of a 50/50 America that turns political discussion into partisan diatribe and moral discourse into moral combat in the "culture-wars." The "50/50 America" terminology is used to describe an electorate split almost 50/50, the slimness of the margin increasing the intensity of the battle.

Six: The promise and perils of economic globalization and the glaring gap between rich and poor throughout the world.

Which brings me to this book. It offers the wrestling reflections of a working minister trying to be a faithful pastor during a time of national crisis and disorienting global change. Both church and nation are trying to discern their identities and their mission at this time of history. I will address the issues of Christian identity in the public square. Can Christians bring moral energy and moral discernment into the public realm without the presumption of moral superiority? Are there moral principles in our Hebrew and Christian foundations that can work for the common good without the taint of theocracy?

The tendency of Christians and churches in our nation is either: 1) to identify their faith with the causes of the political right or left; or 2) to avoid all serious discussion of the place of faith and religious values in the public square. The first is a form of idolatry; the second is a form of moral irresponsibility.

In this book I attempt to bring the values of my spiritual tradition to the public arena. There are essays, sermons, public addresses, and newspaper articles. Part One is primarily essays, though some found their beginnings in sermons. Part Two is mostly sermons, placed in their specific time and circumstance. I hope this book will help Christian pastors, church leaders, and congregations to discover ways they can talk about these issues without adding to the cultural and political rancor all about us. I hope it will build bridges in "50/50" America, a political divide that opens up fissures in churches, communities, friendships, and even marriages. I preached a sermon in July of 2004 called "How to Be Christian in an Election Year." It spoke about how Democrats and Republicans could honor each other and be in constructive conversation. Three different couples came to me and said, "Thanks for the marriage counseling!"

I hope these essays will stir conversations with people of other faiths and of no particular faith who fear that religion in the public square will only lead to theocracy and the loss of religious and personal liberty. And I hope they will address the opposite set of fears in other people of good will that what modernity has bequeathed to us is what John Neuhaus termed "the naked public square,"[3] a society devoid of moral and religious influence, if not openly hostile to religion, or what Stephen L. Carter has called "The Culture of Disbelief,"[4] where religion is trivialized, scorned, and politely escorted from the public square.

Answers to the challenges of this new era lie partly in the past as we carry on conversation with those of past centuries who have struggled with the issues of human nature and the making of a "good society." But new answers must arise. Rowan Williams, Anglican theologian and archbishop of Canterbury, in his book on the Arian controversy in the fourth century when the church struggled to define orthodoxy and heresy, wrote of experiencing orthodoxy "as something still future." Orthodoxy, he says, "continues to be made."[5] So our best answers to the question of moral/spiritual values in the public square are "still future," still "something to be made," made for the urgent realities of our day.

PART ONE

Thinking About Faith and Politics

THE EDUCATION OF A BAPTIST BOY FROM THE SOUTH

I began my life as a Christian in Southern Baptist church life. We prided ourselves as being a "true New Testament church," but as Baptist preacher/theologian Carlyle Marney described us, we were "more Southern than Baptist and more Baptist than Christian." [1]

We were taught to be "in the world but not of it," the "world" seen primarily as a place of sin and temptation. "Sin" was mostly defined in terms of personal sins, primarily sex and alcohol: tasting sex outside marriage and tasting alcohol anywhere. Chastity, not charity, seemed our big concern.

The relationship of "church and state," Christianity and the nation, was full of ambiguity. We proudly held to the Baptist doctrine of "separation of church and state," but that conviction generally issued into political quietism. "God 'n' country" was one word.

Most Baptist churches had the American flag displayed in the sanctuary, a tradition begun in many churches during World War II. We did not know the display of the national flag would be anathema to most Baptist churches around the world, who held minority status in their cultures and zealously guarded the separation of church from state.

Southern Baptists had become in many parts of the South the "majority faith." Someone jokingly called us the "Roman

Catholic Church of the South" because we were the established religion of the region.

So in my growing up years, we Baptists had little argument with the nation and its policies. At the annual summertime Vacation Bible School, we children assembled every day and pledged allegiance to two flags, the Christian flag and the flag of the United States of America. It never occurred to us that there could ever be a conflict between the two allegiances.

Moreover, we had little empathy with those of minority faith status around us: Roman Catholics, Jews, Jehovah's Witnesses, Mormons, and Quakers. We hardly knew who they were. The first time I saw a Catholic make the sign of the cross was in 1957, when a star player on the University of North Carolina basketball team, who had been imported from New York City, made the sign of the cross before every free throw. Because they won the national championship, I wondered whether it worked! Islam and Eastern religions were not on my radar screen at all.

We were also mostly blind to the racism that was so much a part of our social fabric. If the "Deep South" was more famously known for its more overt forms of racism, the "middle south" like my home state North Carolina had softer forms of racism, "softer" at least from our white perspective. We were respectful, genteel, and patronizing toward blacks. But any show of black power sent shivers up our spines and murmurs of righteous indignation about how blacks ought to be grateful for how much progress had been made.

My own parents taught me respect for black people and would not have allowed any racist jokes or racist epithets. My church would have been considered more progressive than many Baptist churches on the race issues. But we, no doubt, embraced the "gradualism" of many white Americans: the affirmation that we needed to make progress toward desegregation and equality but that it must proceed cautiously, slowly. Real slow.

But I still heard racist jokes. I remember with shame going along and laughing with others. I heard whispered jokes about Martin Luther King Jr., jokes made more nervous by his growing influence. And when Dr. King was assassinated while I was in college (a progressive Baptist school, Stetson University), I heard cheers coming from some dormitory windows on the campus. Chills still come as I remember that evening.

Race was the issue that brought a "crisis of faith" to many young Baptists in the 1960s. We saw a crack in the righteousness of our churches. When Southern Baptist churches took an aggressively negative posture toward the Civil Rights movement or hid behind "gradualism," many young people were jolted into critical examination of their faith and their culture.

It was, however, the Vietnam War in the late 1960s that created for my baby boomer age group that wrenching first crisis of conscience. There was no doubt an element of self-preservation at work. The military draft gave deferments to those getting further education, including going to seminaries and divinity schools. There was no small number of theological students who heard the "call" of God a bit clearer with the Vietnam War looming over their shoulders. I was rescued from military service by the double boon of a high lottery number and an admission to seminary. I would like to think that without those protections, I would have filed for conscientious objector status and served my nation in some form of alternative service. But I doubt I would have, mainly because my particular "Baptist" tradition would not have invited me to consider such an option of conscience. By virtue of its history beginning in the Radical Reformation when Anabaptists fought and died for the freedom to dissent and not to serve in the military, my church should have taught me the availability of this path, but it was nowhere to be found in my Southern Baptist faith.

Indeed, it was not unusual at R.A. summer camp (Royal Ambassadors was the Baptist equivalent of Boy Scouts) for an officer of the Armed Forces to have a booth set up to tell about a career in the military.

The crisis of conscience over the Vietnam War intensified as we watched the war on television, saw the carnage of a war never officially approved by Congress, and heard our President lie on national television about the invasion of Cambodia. What other lies had we been told? Who could be trusted?

Such issues came even more to the front as I went to study at Union Theological Seminary in New York City, a famed interdenominational seminary in the "liberal Protestant" tradition (that is, a progressive, ecumenical form of Christianity with an emphasis on social transformation and a rigorous and critical approach to biblical studies and theology). In addition to classic courses in Biblical Studies, Ethics, Church History, and Theology, I took a course with the radical Jesuit priest Daniel Berrigan, who had just been paroled from federal prison to teach at Woodstock College, a Jesuit seminary that in the early 1970s was a part of Union Theological Seminary. Daniel and his brother Phillip had as leaders of the "Catonsville Nine" been convicted of pouring homemade napalm on U.S. draft files. It was a symbolic prophetic act of protest, and as spoken liturgy over this sacrament of conscience Berrigan read aloud in court:

> Our apologies good friends / for the fracture of good order, / the burning of paper / instead of children. [2]

As a Baptist boy I had always been taught that following Jesus was a radical and costly thing to do, but I had never met one like Berrigan, who from Christian conscience had defied his nation's laws and gone to prison. He made me examine at a deeper level than ever before the issues of Christian conscience and the nation. I joined in some forms of war protest but never at the risk of arrest. A good Baptist boy could not go that far.

While at Union I also learned of the different options of relating faith to the public sphere. There was the "resistance theology" of Berrigan and William Stringfellow; there were also the various "liberation theologies" springing up: the Black Liberation Theology of James Cone, the Feminist Liberation Theology of Mary Daly, the South American Liberation Theology of Brazilian theologian Rubem Alves. (I do not deal directly with the issues of feminism and the women's rights movement in this book, but here was another crack in the armor of a "Christian faith," perceived as perfect and invincible. A patriarchal and male-centered church had all too easily supported a society based on male superiority and at times had been the last line of defense of an unjust society. The Equal Rights Amendment, women's ordination, and abortion rights became important issues in this emancipation movement. I as a young male minister had a lot to learn.)

I also was introduced to the "Christian Realism" of Reinhold Niebuhr, Union's most famous theologian. Though he had just died, his spirit and thought permeated the place. He was a "chastened liberal" who thought liberalism did not take into enough consideration the doctrine of sin. But he could not give up the liberal impulse that brought faith issues into the political realm. His calling was to bring Christian values into the public realm to bear upon national policies and national purpose. Our political thought, he argued, had to account for our human capacities both for good and for evil. A famous quote of Niebuhr's says that "man's capacity for justice makes democracy possible; but man's inclination to injustice makes democracy necessary."[3] I still find his theological and intellectual work compelling.

My Ph.D. dissertation considered the relationship of Christ and social structures as I studied the Social Gospel of Walter Rauschenbush, the Christian Realism of Niebuhr, the Conservative Political Philosophy of Eric Voegelin, the Resistance Theology of Berrigan and Stringfellow, and the Black Liberation Theology of James Cone. I do not know why these things mattered so much to me except that I was trying to understand and resolve the uneasy peace my Baptist faith had made with the "powers that be." How does one exercise Christian calling in relation to one's nation? The Baptist church in the South had for all its warnings about the sinful "world" become captive to its culture, "more Southern than Baptist and more Baptist than Christian."

My calling as a pastor to congregations led me to be pastor of two seminary-related congregations, Crescent Hill Baptist in Louisville, Kentucky (1981–1992) and Broadway Baptist in Fort Worth, Texas (1992–1999). These were the years of the fundamentalist takeover of the Southern Baptist Convention and its agencies, including the seminaries. The Religious Right had shown its muscle, and our seminaries were being utterly changed.

Progressive thought in Southern Baptist life went into exile. During this same era most Baptists in the South shifted from the Democratic Party to the Republican Party. Though Jimmy Carter and Bill Clinton were Southern Baptists, most Southern Baptists supported Ronald Reagan and the two Presidents Bush. Conservative political analyst Kevin Phillips in his recent book, *American Theocracy*, documents and reflects upon the radicalized religion of the Right, the "southernization" of American politics, the "theologization" of American politics, and the "reorganization of the Republican Party around religion," making it America's first religious party. He makes the changes in the Southern Baptist Convention a central case study. [4]

My theological interests led me often through the years to engage Christian faith with social and political issues. I would venture out on a limb, get bloodied a bit, retreat for a while, return to other important facets of the Christian faith—personal faith, biblical exposition, spiritual guidance—then venture out again, bolder than some, more timid than others. I have sought throughout my life some healthy and faithful balance.

A Christian minister is called to "push the envelope," prodding his or her congregation to deeper thinking and more faithful action. Since most ministers are also driven by our inordinate need to be loved by *everybody*, this presents a tiny little problem. But unless we are willing to do this difficult, sometimes painful, work, Christianity will become indistinguishable from its culture, the "bland leading the bland." It is all too easy to shunt aside the fact that the Jesus we are called to follow was rejected by most, especially by the political and religious elite, and was executed as a common criminal on a Roman gallows.

There is something about the course of Jesus' life that should give us a hint that following Jesus just might place us at some variance with our culture. As Flannery O' Connor paraphrased Jesus: "You shall know the truth, and the truth shall make you odd." [5] I think I've spent most of my life trying not to be odd.

There is little in this book that I have not tried to say to my congregation and community. There is little in this book that I have said easily. I have often asked, "Okay, God, why have I, a

Southern boy who needs the adoration of almost everybody, taken up a calling that demands that I say things that make almost everybody uncomfortable at one time or another and that strains relationships with those of my congregation who, by the way, pay my salary?"

For the last six years, my efforts have been sustained by a remarkable congregation, Myers Park Baptist Church, whose church covenant affirms that we are "open to all new light" and says boldly that we "accept controversy as a reality of life together and an opportunity for growth toward maturity." One of its core stated values is the "freedom of the pulpit," which supports and encourages its ministers to challenge the congregation and community. My predecessors in its pulpit have not squandered the opportunity of such rare freedom, and if I enjoy any freedom in the pulpit—and I have more than I *enjoy*—it is because these preachers and this congregation have nurtured religious liberty and the unhindered search for truth.

My congregation, a predominantly privileged and white congregation, represents a fair sample of our 50/50 America, with a generous offering of people from the political and Religious Right and the political and Religious Left. There are also the many in the uncomfortable middle. I hope that my ongoing conversations with them will be of help to others who are trying to bridge the gulf between Left and Right.

Ours is a time of national and global crisis. "Crisis" may seem like too ominous a word to some. I mean the word in its biblical sense: a time of important *decision* where great good and great ill are at stake. I mean it in the sense of the two-character Chinese pictograph for the word "crisis": the joining of signs for "danger" and "opportunity."

Can our nation of high ideals and great spiritual resources become as "good" a nation as it aspires to be? Can we be so as the world's great superpower in an era of falling towers?

CHAPTER TWO

AMERICA AND PROVIDENCE

From "City on a Hill" to "An Almost Chosen People" to Servant of the "God Beyond God" in the Community of Nations

The word "Providence" has been liberally sprinkled throughout public discourse about America for its whole history. "Providence" is a word used to describe God's superintendence of the world. Theologians have sought to describe a God who looks over the welfare of the entire world while at the same time looking after the welfare of every person and creature in it. God's "eye is on the sparrow" and on the nations and on me. The God of Providence is the creator of the world and its sustainer and renewer.

Hebrew and Christian scriptures have pictured a God who relates to the nations in a variety of ways. Here is an all too brief summary.

1. God uses nations to achieve the moral goods of justice, mercy, stability, freedom, and peace.

2. God gives to all nations and peoples the moral capacity for the exercise of these civic virtues and judges nations based upon their approximation of them.

3. God uses as instruments of the divine purpose even nations who do not acknowledge God. So, for example, Cyrus the Persian king is variously called "servant," "shepherd," and "anointed one" of the Lord as he delivers the Hebrew people home from Babylonian captivity (Isa. 44–45).

4. Nations serve the minimal function of preserving order and executing justice in a chaotic and sinful world (Rom. 13).

5. God "laughs at" the nations who strut as gods upon the earth (Ps. 2).

6. A nation's care for the poor, hungry, weak, and vulnerable is the key to how they will be finally judged. Jesus' parable about the Last Judgment is about the way nations are judged (Matt. 25: 31-46).

7. There are times God's mercy and forgiveness is at work sparing nations and giving them a new start (Jonah).

From its beginnings, America has seen itself as a "chosen nation," a nation given a unique mission in the world. "Providence" and America's experiment in democracy have been joined. This chapter will explore the idea of national "chosenness," its strengths and its dangers, and consider how best to speak such language today.

America has always lived with a sense of national purpose, of being a part of the Divine Providence, of having a "mission" in the world, whether that mission was conceived of in secular or religious terms.

John Winthrop, newly elected governor of the Massachusetts Bay Colony, was still en route to America aboard the *Arabella* when he wrote:

> We shall find that the God of Israel is among us.... For we must consider that we shall be as a city on a hill, the eyes of all people are upon us. [1]

The imagery came from the Bible in Hebrew scriptures: "I will give you as a light to the nations" (Isa. 49:6) and in the Gospels in Jesus' Sermon on the Mount: "You are the light of the world. A city set on a hill cannot be hid" (Matt. 5:14).

From the beginning there were two major strands of American "messianism," the belief that America had a unique mission in the world. Messianism is a nation's sense of being chosen by God and called to a particular historical purpose. It may take religious form as in America as the "New Israel" or a more secular form as America's mission to spread democracy and advance freedom. (It can take a radically secular form as in Communism's mission to bring in a "classless society.")

The first strand of American messianism was New England Puritanism. America was the "New Israel" formed to establish God's kingdom on earth. In his important work *The Kingdom of God in America*, H. Richard Niebuhr traced the successive eras of this theo-political dream:

1. "The Sovereignty of God": the Puritan ideal of America as the New Israel;

2. "The Kingdom of Christ": revivalism's dream of transformed individuals leading to a transformed society;

3. "The Coming Kingdom": the Social Gospel's challenge of a "Christianized" social order based on the social principles of Jesus. [2] (The regeneration of the individual was not enough; we needed community action to transform society.)

The vitalizing character of American Christianity has been its fervent belief that God's kingdom was meant for *earth*.

It is crucial to note here that the city on a hill metaphor used by Winthrop was carefully placed within a *covenant-theology* that was highly conditional: if America followed God's precepts, the nation would prosper and be a shining light to the world. If not, the failings of this "city on a hill" would be seen and judged by all the world. The image of a nation on trial by God before all the world was a familiar theme for the Hebrew prophets. This fuller excerpt from Winthrop's famous sermon shows the conditionality of its covenant context:

Now the only way...to provide for our posterity is to follow the counsel of Micah: to do justly, to love mercy, to walk humbly with our God. For this end, we must be knit together in this work as one man....For we must consider that we shall be as a city upon a hill, the eyes of all people are upon us. So that if we shall deal falsely with our God in this work we have undertaken, and so cause Him to withdraw His present help from us, we shall be made a story and a by-word through the world: we shall open the mouths of enemies to speak evil of the ways of God and all professors for God's sake; we shall shame the faces of many of God's worthy servants, and cause their prayers to be turned into curses upon us, till we be consumed out of the good land whither we are going. [3]

The secular strand of American messianism came from the Enlightenment and was the basis for the great American experiment of democracy. America was the "New Adam" beginning a new chapter in the social progress of humanity. In *Common Sense*, the famous Enlightenment deist Thomas Paine wrote, "We have it in our power to begin the world all over again." A pretty heady assessment. Ronald Reagan loved to use this line because of its optimism, but some writers—including George Will—have noted that we can scarcely imagine a less conservative notion. (Something brand new in history?)

These two strands were often blended as one. Reinhold Niebuhr, perhaps America's premier theologian of the mid-twentieth century, wrote:

Like Israel of old we were a messianic nation from our birth. The Declaration of Independence and our Constitution defined the mission. We were born to exemplify the virtues of democracy and extend the frontiers of the principles of self-government throughout the world. [4]

Both strands of American "chosenness" were infected with what some have called American "exceptionalism": America would succeed where other nations had failed through the centuries because of the superiority of our mission and our national character. The "American Adam"[5] would escape the fate of the original Adam.

Our nation wants the blessing—as most people do—but not the responsibility. After the Revolutionary War, the "city on a hill" metaphor was severed from its covenantal origins. We were a glorious light to the benighted world. Nowhere was there the picture that as a nation on a hill we were being watched by God and the nations to see what kind of people we would become. Gerhard Sauter calls this development "a metaphor torn in half."[6]

But there was also from the beginning mixed into our messianism a theological and political "realism" about human nature that tempered our idealism and helped keep our messianism from losing its head. Reading classical literature and the Bible, our founders pondered whether we could escape the fate of earlier nations. Reinhold Niebuhr was a theological champion of such realism in the twentieth century, reminding us of the inescapable presence of human sin. Historian Arthur Schlesinger, an admirer of Reinhold Niebuhr, expressed this tension in American life as "the warfare between realism and messianism, between experiment and destiny."[7] America as an "experiment" recognized its commonality with humanity past and present and had a sober hope of our success in this new venture. On the other side, America as a "chosen people," with the destiny of God on its side, was tempted to think it would indeed start something brand-new in the history of the world. Schlesinger, who comes down clearly on the side of realism, writes:

> For Messianism is an illusion. No nation is sacred and unique, the United States or any other. All nations are immediate to God. America, like every country, has interests real and fictitious, concerns generous and selfish, motives honorable and squalid. Providence has not set Americans apart from lesser breeds. We too are a part of history's seamless web.[8]

Before the American Revolution John Adams, flirting with messianism, said:

> I always consider the settlement of America with reverence, as the opening of a grand scheme and design in Providence for the illumination of the ignorant and the emancipation of the slavish part of mankind all over the earth. [9]

But he deleted this sentence before he published the paper, "Dissertation on the Canon and Feudal Law." Later in the 1780s, he concluded that there was "no special providence for Americans, and their nature is the same with that of others." [10]

The genius of the American experiment is that it has lived in the creative tension between realism and messianism, experiment and destiny. To use theological terms, it recognized the constraints of humanity and its stubborn flaws, but it also believed that God could do a new thing in history and that America could be part of it. There was a dream of a new age dawning, but this dream was tempered by the recognition that we are cut from the same cloth as all humanity. We have seen at times the tension collapse, sometimes in favor of untempered messianism, other times in favor of a cynicism about human and national potentialities.

In the early nineteenth century we saw an untempered American messianism. We were God's "elect nation" or "redeemer nation." William Gilpin, the famous journalist who coined the phrase "Manifest Destiny," wrote these words, read to the Senate in 1846:

> The *untransacted* destiny of the American people is to subdue the continent—to rush over this vast field to the Pacific Ocean—to animate the many hundred millions of its people, and to cheer them upward . . . to teach old nations a new civilization—to conform the destiny of the human race. [11]

Throughout our history, presidents, liberal and conservative, have embraced our self-identification as a chosen nation, as a nation grasped by God's destiny for the human race, but this notion becomes dangerous if we forget the limitations of humanity, which we share with all.

Abraham Lincoln saw our nation with a mission to the world: to further humanity's struggle toward freedom. But this sense of national mission had the conditionality of the earlier Puritan covenantal theology. In his address to Congress, December 1, 1862, he proposed a political solution to end slavery and save the Union—the gradual emancipation of the slaves. We must, he said, "disenthrall" ourselves from the dogmas of the past:

> Fellow-citizens, we cannot escape history. . . . The fiery trial through which we pass, will light us down, in honor or dishonor. . . . We know how to save the Union. . . . In *giving* freedom to the *slave*, we *assure* freedom to the free. . . . We shall nobly save, or meanly lose, the last best, hope of earth. [12]

Lincoln believed in America's unique mission in the world, but his sense of national mission bowed beneath a finally inscrutable Providence. We could not claim to know perfectly the mind of God or claim perfectly to do God's will. So in his address to the New Jersey Senate, February 21, 1861, he spoke of his hope in the present travail to be:

> an humble instrument in the hands of the Almighty and of this his *almost chosen people* . . . [13]

His intellectual and spiritual reserve in naming us as God's "almost chosen people" was something needed then and is something newly needed in our age of absolutist politics and absolutist religion. It combined idealism and realism, experiment and destiny.

We as a nation have in the past two decades moved from being one of the strongest nations on earth with a mission to exemplify and spread democracy to being the singular superpower on earth. The new status carries with it a more terrible responsibility and the moral crucible of the ambiguity of power.

Reinhold Niebuhr was a prophet not only to his time but also to ours when he helped America in the 1950s come to terms with its new place of power in the world following World War II. In

1958, Niebuhr pondered the "transformation" of the nation and its original sense of mission to its present sense of responsibility as leader of the free nations:

> This transformation meant the gradual adjustment of the original sense of mission—its messianic or quasi-messianic consciousness of being the initiator and bearer of the principles of constitutional democracy ("the last best hope of earth")—to the responsibilities of power exercised as a nation as one of the two hegemonous nations of earth [USA and USSR]. [14]

Today, close to fifty years later, our nation is now the world's only superpower. Its military budget is greater than that of all the other nations of the world combined. [15] Its moral responsibilities and the moral hazards it inevitably faces as a nation with such power have dramatically increased.

How can we speak of our "chosenness" or our "mission" in our world today where chosenness and mission can become the justification for international terrorism and preemptive war? Can a people's chosenness come to terms with the ambiguity of power? Again Niebuhr, now in 1963:

> A sense of mission is not an unmixed blessing. A sense of mission may be a source of confusion when it tempts nations with a messianic consciousness to hide the inevitable vital impulses of collective existence, chiefly the will to power, under the veil of its ideal purposes. Such nations are inclined to pretend that they have triumphed over the baser impulses and to be wholly devoted to ideal ends. [16]

My apprehensiveness about our nation today is that our idealism may hide from us the perennial moral ambiguity of the exercise of power, made even more dangerous by our prodigious power. If we live with a false innocence, believing that we are morally and spiritually different from, or better than, other peoples of the world, we set ourselves up for a terrible fall. Our form of government may be morally better than other forms, e.g., totalitarian or repressive governments, but we are not angels and they are not demons. There is human evil that must be fought, but we fight knowing our capacities for evil and our enemy's capacity for good.

Reinhold Niebuhr saw that democratic nations might shrink from the use of power because any use of power is in his words "morally hazardous." But they, as all nations, can be tempted to too great a power. Nations then wrestle with contradictory temptations:

> They may be tempted to flee the responsibilities of their power or refuse to develop their potentialities. But they may also refuse to recognize the limits of their possibilities and seek greater power than is given to mortals. [17]

In theological terms, these are, respectively, the temptations of sloth and pride. The wrong use of a nation's power, he says:

> is always due to some failure to recognize the limits of [the human] capacities of power, wisdom and virtue. [18]

Hence the wise nation submits itself:

> to a sense of awe before the vastness of the historical drama in which we are jointly involved; to a sense of modesty about the virtue, wisdom and power available to us for the resolution of its perplexities; to a sense of contrition about the common human frailties and foibles which lie at the foundation of both the enemy's demonry and our vanities; and to a sense of gratitude for the divine mercies which are promised to those who humble themselves. [19]

Reinhold Niebuhr today would be, I think, as clear-eyed in his naming of jihadism as a human evil as he was in naming Communism as a human evil during the Cold War. But this evil is a human evil that lurks in our souls too.

What can we say of our nation today? A City on a Hill? An Almost Chosen Nation? Our power has led us to the precipice of pride. In his Second Inaugural Address, President Bush said:

23

We go forward with complete confidence in the eventual triumph of freedom.

Then he carefully added:

Not *because we consider ourselves a chosen nation*; God moves and chooses as He wills. We have confidence because freedom is the perennial hope of mankind. (emphasis mine)

But in other speeches he has been given to a more grandiose picture of America. On September 14, 2001, in the National Cathedral he said:

But our responsibility to history is already clear: to answer these attacks and rid the world of evil.

And in his State of the Union address, January 28, 2003, as we were mobilizing for war in Iraq he said to the nation:

Once again, we are called to defend the safety of our people, and the hopes of all mankind. And we accept this responsibility.... We do not know—we do not claim to know all the ways of Providence, yet we can trust in them, placing our confidence in the loving God behind all of life, and all of history. May he guide us now. And may God continue to bless the United States of America.

The war began fifty days later, March 19, 2003.

America lives with the promise and peril of what Robert Bellah has termed "civil religion"—defined by Gerhard Sauter as "the transfer of religious symbols into national self-understanding." [20]

The promise of civil religion is its belief that we can be about the work of God in history. Such belief has given us the moral vision and moral energy to defeat tyranny, establish democracy, end slavery, and grant women political equality. The peril of civil religion is that it can lead a nation to claim too much, to national self-righteousness, and to a blindness to its own human weak-nesses.

How might we then speak of our nation and God in the same breath today? Lincoln's "almost chosen people" is a beautifully nuanced phrase that lives in the tension between "experiment" and "destiny."

Here is how I would phrase it for the demands of our days: *The United States is a servant-nation of the "God beyond God" in the community of nations.*

Servant-nation is a more modest phrase than "elect-nation" or "chosen-nation," which have been used to describe us in our past. As a servant-nation we bow beneath the transcendent God, knowing we have only a human measure of power, wisdom, and goodness. We seek to champion the values we perceive are God's values: justice, equality, freedom, mercy, stability, and peace. But we always acknowledge that our best successes are but approxi-mations of God's will.

The God we seek to serve is the "God beyond God." This is Paul Tillich's phrase. The true God is the One beyond the "God" of our religions, philosophies, ethnicities, and nations, though present in them. Perhaps Christians should spell God's name "G-d" to mark our reverence, much as Jews refuse to speak or spell their holy name for God: YHWH. We should exercise a holy reticence when speaking God's name in public discourse. And if we speak of God's will it should be with Abraham Lincoln's qualification: as it "appears" to me. (See page 30.)

How would I describe the character of "God"? It is a God whose great work is reconciliation and who "promised to judge and to save in reconciling the world."[21] At some moments of his-tory our nation will experience God's saving action, at other times God's judging action.

Paul D. Hanson of Harvard in his magisterial work on the Jewish and Christian scriptures, *The People Called*, writes: "Some (myself included) would argue that a parochial version of Christianity that promises divine grace apart from confession and repentance, and that promulgates the notion of a particular nation as enjoying a privileged place in God's favor, is a betrayal

of the biblical tradition that is at the heart of the Christian her-
itage, a tradition that develops a universal mission of divine justice and peace." [22]

Finally, we take our place in the community of nations who are
more like us than unlike us and who have as much to give us as
to receive from us. If we fail in our "mission" in the world this
early twenty-first century, it will be from an overestimation of our
own power, wisdom, and goodness and from an underestimation
of these virtues in other peoples. That is, it will come from our
pride, which as the wisdom of the Bible says, "goeth before a fall"
(Prov. 16:18 KJV).

CHAPTER THREE

THE SPIRITUAL AND POLITICAL VIRTUE OF REVERENCE

Abraham Lincoln as an American Exemplar

They come to me and talk about God's will
In righteous deputations and platoons,
Day after day, laymen and ministers.
They write me Prayers From Twenty Million Souls
Defining me God's will and Horace Greeley's.
God's will is General This and General That,
God's will is those poor colored fellows' will,
It is the will of the Chicago churches,
It is this man's and his worst enemy's.
But all of them are sure they know God's will.
I am the only man who does not know it.

And, yet, if it is probable that God
Should, and so very clearly, state His will
To others, on a point of my own duty,
It might be thought he would reveal it me
Directly, more especially as I
So earnestly desire to know His will.
—Abraham Lincoln paraphrase by Stephen Vincent
Benét in "John Brown's Body"

L et me speak of reverence as a spiritual and political virtue and of Abraham Lincoln as an American exemplar, a light in our darkened skies. In his famous poem of 1920, "The Second Coming," W. B. Yeats pictured the loss of reverence in our modern world:

> Things fall apart; The centre cannot hold. [1]

In 2001, on the eve of 9/11 and the coming war on terrorism and war in Iraq, University of Texas philosopher Robert Woodruff published a small but important book, *Reverence: Renewing a Forgotten Virtue*. In it he traces a crucial cross-cultural virtue found in all true religions and a bedrock virtue of ancient Greece and China: Reverence. He writes:

> Reverence is an ancient virtue that survives among us in half-forgotten patterns of civility, in moments of inarticulate awe, and in nostalgia for the lost ways of traditional cultures....Reverence begins in a deep understanding of human limitations. [2]

Simply put, reverence is the virtue that "keeps human beings from trying to act like gods." Religion becomes irreverent when it no longer bows before the Holy, or when it presumes to know too completely the mind of God. Government becomes irreverent when it denies the transcendent and tries to become the ultimate realm—as in Communism. Or when it, sure of its own goodness, presumes it is doing God's will—America's temptation. Woodruff defines reverence as "the well developed capacity to have the feelings of awe, respect, and shame when these are the right feelings to have." [3] To be sure, awe, respect, and shame can be manipulated and used for ill. Religion can manipulate awe, government can manipulate respect, and the family can manipulate shame. (Religion can manipulate all three!) But rightly developed, these build both personal character and the good society.

Awe is the feeling we have when we stand before something greater than we are, something we cannot control.

Respect is the honor we pay to other people because they are people of worth. An irreverent person displays contempt and disrespect for others, especially those perceived as weaker.

Shame is what we feel when we have broken our deepest standards, betrayed our deepest values.

Without reverence, these three—religion, government, and family—can turn into killers. With reverence, these most vital human institutions serve to preserve and enrich life. Woodruff sums up: "Reverence runs across religions and even outside them through the fabric of any community, however secular. We may be divided from one another by our beliefs, but never by reverence. If you desire peace in the world, do not pray that everyone share your beliefs. Pray instead that all may be reverent." [4]

I know no greater American exemplar of reverence as a political and spiritual virtue than Abraham Lincoln. His life and his speeches have always struck me as a most extraordinary combination of conviction and humility. Woodruff has given me a new way to name this quality.

A recent award-winning book by Allen Guelzo, *Abraham Lincoln: Redeemer President*, gives us a deeper insight into Lincoln's life and character—and into his quality of reverence. [5] Lincoln's early religious life was in his father's church, a rigidly strict Calvinistic Baptist Church: in Kentucky, the Little Mount Separate Baptist Church; and in Indiana, the Little Pigeon Creek Baptist Church. It appears that Abraham never took to this narrow form of Christianity, though it planted a deep faith in the Providence of God, something that later would be an enormous resource. [6]

Lincoln was enamored with Enlightenment thought; as a young man he wrote what he titled "A Little Book on Infidelity," which voiced his skepticism about traditional church doctrines. His friends, fearing that the book might tarnish his reputation and career, took it from him and burned it. As quoted in Guelzo, in 1846 he wrote a friend, "Probably it is my lot to go on in a twilight, feeling and reasoning my way through life, as questioning, doubting Thomas did." [7]

In his early political career he adopted Whig politics and Whig religion; that is, classical economic liberalism that embraced the good of market economics, and an evangelical Protestant belief that religiously inspired personal virtues were good for the nation as well as the person.

But the great tests of his personal and political life led him to a deepening sense of the Providence of God active in the world, that is, into growing reverence. The personal tests were his mother's death when he was nine, the tragic death of His fiancée, Ann Rutledge, and later, when married, the deaths of two of his children. The political test was having to lead a nation during the Civil War. Guelzo writes: "Lincoln...started in the 1830s from a position of unorthodoxy not much different from Jefferson's, but throughout his life he increasingly wrapped his political ideas around religious themes, appealing at the very end to a mysterious providence whose inscrutable and irresistible workings both baffled and comforted him."[8]

Lincoln's reverence was that he trusted in God's Providence without presuming to know it. In a letter to English Quaker Eliza Gurney, he wrote that if he failed in his mission to preserve the Union: "I must believe that for some purpose unknown to me, He wills it otherwise...and we must believe that He permits it for some wise purpose of his own, mysterious and unknown to us; and though with our limited understandings we may not be able to comprehend it, yet we cannot but believe it, that *he who made the world still governs it.*"[9] (Emphasis mine.)

He believed that God was active on behalf of good, but he did not presume to know how God was at work or that he, Lincoln, was doing God's will. He chided ministers who came proclaiming God's will for him as president: "I hope it will not be irreverent for me to say that if it is probable that God would reveal his will to others, on a point so connected with my duty, it might be supposed he would reveal it directly to me."[10]

When liberal clergy from Chicago came to lobby him to sign an emancipation proclamation, Lincoln said, "Whatever shall appear to me to be God's will I will do."[11] The word "appear" is crucial. Lincoln would always act on what he perceived to be God's will, but he always knew it was his perception.

In the middle of war, the fate of the Union in the balance, Lincoln pondered whether to deliver the Emancipation Proclamation. He did something his earlier, more deist, faith would not have allowed. He made a promise to himself and to his "Maker" that if the Union forces won the battle of Antietam he would take it as a sign to move forward. [12] The battle was won and the Emancipation Proclamation was signed. He is quoted saying to his cabinet: "This might seem strange," but "God had decided the question in favor of the slaves." [13]

Lincoln's combination of conviction and humility was evident in a famous address to Republicans on February 27, 1860, at the Cooper Union. Lincoln concluded with these words, written in capital letters:

LET US HAVE FAITH THAT RIGHT MAKES MIGHT, AND IN THAT FAITH LET US, TO THE END, DARE TO DO OUR DUTY AS WE UNDERSTAND IT.

The conviction: "that right makes might" and that we "dare to do our duty"; the humility: "as we understand it." Such a spirit was later echoed in his Second Inaugural Address: "With firmness in the right *as God gives us to see the right*, let us strive on to finish the work we are in." (Emphasis mine.)

Lincoln believed slavery was wrong and a great evil: "If slavery is not wrong, nothing is wrong." But he never demonized the South or Southerners. He did not engage in "moral splitting" where he was the righteous one and others were evil. He was able, in the words of William Lee Miller, "to make a moral argument without being moralistic." [14] He opposed slavery, but he avoided the moral absolutism of leading abolitionists even as he joined in their moral purpose.

Lincoln believed our nation's great mission was in the struggle for liberty, but he was careful not to identify our nation with the kingdom of God, or claim, as many a politician or preacher might, that America was God's chosen people. We were, as noted above, God's "almost chosen people":

> I shall be most happy indeed if I shall be an humble instrument in the hands of the Almighty, and of this, his almost chosen people, for perpetuating the object of that great struggle. [15]

In his First Inaugural Address, he swore an oath he took to be an oath to God: to defend and protect the Constitution—which included its enforcement in all parts of the United States—and to preserve the Union. His tone was conciliatory:

> We are not enemies, but friends. We must not be enemies. Though passion may have strained, it must not break our bonds of affection.

And he appealed to the best in every American, that we might be touched, to use his great phrase, "by the better angels of our nature." [16]

In his famous Gettysburg Address, Lincoln expressed a reverent gratitude for the sacrifices of the soldiers and for the ideal for which they and their forebears had fought:

> a new nation, conceived in liberty and dedicated to the proposition that all men are created equal. [17]

When he ran for reelection, he did so with the equanimity of one who placed his life and political career into God's hands. His close friend, Leonard Swett, said:

> If he was elected, he seemed to believe that no person, or class of people, could ever have defeated him, and if defeated, he believed nothing could ever have elected him. [18]

Then in his Second Inaugural speech, a theological and political masterpiece, he addressed the whole nation with that combination of conviction and humility, strength and mercy—the qualities of reverence:

Neither party expected for the war, the magnitude, or the duration, which it has already attained....Each looked for an easier triumph, and a result less fundamental and astounding.
Both read the same Bible, and pray to the same God; and each
invokes His aid against the other....The prayers of both could
not be answered; that of neither has been answered fully. The
Almighty has His own purposes....With malice toward none;
with charity for all; with firmness in the right, as God gives us
to see the right, let us strive on to finish the work we are in; to
bind up the nation's wounds; to care for him who shall have
borne the battle, and for his widow, and his orphan— to do all
which may achieve and cherish a just, and a lasting peace,
among ourselves, and with all nations. [19]

It was Lincoln's deep faith in the workings of Providence, combined with his theological and intellectual modesty about our
capacity to know this Providence, that helped him accomplish
his two great goals: end slavery and preserve the Union. [20]

Lincoln's reverence has, for me, deep resonance with King
David of ancient Israel. The scene is civil war afoot in David's
great kingdom, led by his own son Absalom. David is fleeing the
capital city, Jerusalem. He meets his two main priests carrying
with them the ark of the covenant. The ark was the chest that
contained the Ten Commandments. It was the symbol of the
divine protection of God. It was like the flag, the Bible, and the
Constitution all rolled up into one. It was sometimes carried into
battle invoking the divine protection. But David stops the priests
and says:

> Carry the ark of God back into the city. If I find favor in the
> eyes of the LORD, he will bring me back and let me see both it
> and the place where it stays. But if he says, "I take no pleasure
> in you," here I am, let him do to me what seems good to him.
> (2 Sam. 15:25-26)

Imagine a U.S. president whose nation is under attack about to
go on national television. The advisors have carefully placed a

Bible on his desk, next to his hand. The President says, "No, take it away. If God is for us we will prevail. If not, we will not."

One more episode. David is still in flight. A man named Shimei shows up and begins to run alongside David, shouting taunts and accusations, even throwing stones at him. (He probably worked for the *Jerusalem Post*.) David's men come and say to David, "Let us go take off his head." But David says: "Let him alone, and let him curse; for the LORD has bidden him. It may be that…the LORD will repay me with good for this cursing" (2 Sam. 16:11-12). This is not how presidents tend to treat the White House press corps.

Lincoln and David knew something greater was at work, greater than themselves or their nation. This is reverence as a spiritual and political virtue. It is what Jesus displayed when, facing his own arrest and execution, he prayed:

> Abba, Father, for you all things are possible; remove this cup from me; yet, not what I want, but what you want. (Mark 14:36)

In our current age of irreverent religion and irreverent politics, where, as Yeats puts it in "The Second Coming," "The best lack all conviction, while the worst/Are full of passionate intensity," may we be given a truer reverence.

CHAPTER FOUR

THE PROMISE OF POST-CONSTANTINIAN CHRISTIANITY

A "Free Church" Perspective

Despite present attempts of Christian fundamentalists to recreate a "Christian society" or reconstitute "Christendom," we are entering an era that we could call post-Constantinian Christianity. This may be a shock to the psyche of many Christians in the West who have grown up with some historical sense of living in a "Christian culture," but it can be seen as a time of great promise. The church may rediscover its calling to be the church in the world and not the chaplain to a semi-Christian society.

Constantine was the emperor of Rome in the early fourth century. Tradition records that he received a vision from heaven before a crucial battle and interpreted this vision as God's promise of victory. His conversion to Christianity led to Christianity becoming the official religion of the empire. To many Christians this must have seemed like a miracle. Christianity had "won," and they were free from persecution. But every victory has its defeats.

After Constantine's "vision" on the Milvian bridge and his victory over his rival Maxentius, the Christian symbol of the Chi Rho, formed with the first two letters of *Christos*, became the military emblem of the empire. With the power of Christ, he would conquer.

Constantine thought Christianity would be the "cement of the Empire," so when great discord broke out over theology in the church, Constantine interposed to settle the disputes. He called and presided over the Council of Nicea, the first "Ecumenical Council." The line between orthodoxy and heresy was clearly drawn and heretics became enemies of the state as well as the church.

The joining of church and state—what some call "Constantinianism"—was a fateful step, with no doubt some temporary good. But now the formula was set: The state defended, financed, and controlled the church; the church was captive to the state. Christianity and culture were virtually indistinguishable. The goal was "Christendom." Today we are entering a post-Constantinian age. We should greet it, not grieve it.

The "free-church" tradition may help us to see the promise in this bewildering time of transition. What is a shock to some Christian traditions should look more like normality for those in the free-church tradition. So let's take a "free-church look" at the current situation.

Perhaps the most formative free-church theologian of our time has been Mennonite John Howard Yoder. What he likes to call the "free church" tradition has been variously termed "believers' church" (Max Weber), "Radical Reformation" (George H. Williams), and "baptist" (James William McClendon). In the past, some called themselves "brethren." Today representatives of the tradition include a menagerie of folks: Baptists, Mennonites, Quakers, Unitarians, Congregationalists, and many Pentecostals.

These groups have varying theologies but share a belief in the separation of church and state and a critical posture toward what they have identified as one of the most crucial errors of the church: Constantinianism, that fateful joining of church and state from the time of the conversion of Constantine.

John Howard Yoder says that the church's relationship to the "powers that be" involves a two-fold calling: the first is to *con-*

strain the powers to be modest. The state is not God; it is a human instrument to promote human welfare. Thus the church should never sanctify the state. The second is to *resist the powers* when they refuse their modest calling, when they assert their independence from God or try to be like God.[1] The church in the West has in its Constantinian arrangement sanctified the state and identified itself with powers that be rather than exercising its duty of "calling these powers to modesty and resisting their recurrent rebellion."[2]

As Yoder traces the various iterations of this error,[3] there was the original "Constantinianism" of the church's relationship with the Roman Empire and Holy Roman Empire. Then there was the "neo-Constantinianism" of the Protestant Reformation as the church identified with the particular nation-state in which it lived. The Puritan experiment in colonial New England made this error as it tried a new kind of theocracy and identified itself as the New Israel and as God's Chosen People. The first "Baptist" of America, Roger Williams, was banished from the Massachusetts Bay Colony because he resisted this theocraticizing impulse. Ironically, if he were to come back today and visit many of the more famous Baptist churches, like Jerry Falwell's Thomas Road Baptist Church, he'd say: "This looks more like the bunch who threw me out of the Massachusetts Bay Colony than the one I tried to start in Rhode Island!"

Then there was the "neo-neo-Constantinianism" of the nineteenth and early twentieth century when the church blessed its society as a "Christian society." Then there was the church's blessing of its secular society as a morally evolved society, what Yoder calls "neo-neo-neo-Constantinianism." Then there was the church's support of political revolution in some Third-World countries, identifying itself with the movement to overthrow unjust regimes by whatever means necessary, what Yoder calls "neo-neo-neo-neo-Constantinianism"!

The dilemma of the church is that in its rightful effort to aid in the transformation of society, it has sometimes given up its primary calling to witness to the particularity of the message and way of Jesus, whom it calls "Lord." And in its effort to be "effective," to make an "impact," it has accepted the power, blessing, and financial support of the state in exchange for its subservience to the state. The church has been successful and safe and silent.

The free-church witness has through the centuries been a prophetic warning about the dangers of Constantinianism. The twenty-first century is witnessing two colliding realities: 1) The "de-Constantinization" of the church and society in which the church is "disestablished"; and 2) The zealous attempt at "re-Constantinization" as fundamentalists of various religions try to "resacralize" society. The current attempts of conservative politics and conservative religion in America to refashion America as a "Christian nation" is but a new surge in Constantinian Christianity, what we might call after Yoder's scenario "neo-neo-neo-neo-neo-Constantinianism" or "Constantinianism x 5."

In Yoder's mind, the church should not mourn the passing of Constantinian Christianity, nor try to reinstate it, but rather find in this new era the possibility of a new birth of the church:

> How then do we face deconstantinization? If we meet it as just another turn of the inscrutable screw of providence, just one more chance to state the Constantinian position in new terms, then the judgment that has already begun will sweep us along in the collapse of the culture for which we boast that we are responsible. But if we have an ear to hear what the Spirit says to the churches, if we let ourselves be led out of the inferiority complex that the theologies of the Reformation have thus far imposed on free church thought...we are in the same essentially missionary situation, the same minority status as the church in Sri Lanka or Colombia; if we believe that the free church, and not the "free world," is the primary bearer of God's banner, the fullness of the One who fills all in all, if we face deconstantinization not as just another dirty trick of destiny but as the overdue providential unveiling of a pernicious error; then it may be given to us, even in the twentieth century, to be the church. For what more could we ask?[4]

What the church might offer in this post-Constantinian age is the distinctive voice of Jesus. Here are, following Yoder, some marks of Jesus' voice:

1) "The sword is not the source of creativity."[5] Jesus refused the use of violence to further his mission.

2) "There are other more useful ways to contribute to the course of society than attempting to 'rule.'"[6] Medieval society was "Christianized" less by the power of princes than by the "quiet minority of the monastic movements." It is easy to ignore the words of Jesus: "The kings of the nations rule over them, but you shall not do that, you shall be one another's servants, because I came as a servant."[7]

3) Civilization should be evaluated "not by the success of its armies but by how it treated the poor and the foreigner, how it tilled the soil."[8]

4) Violence, brutality, and deceit are particular forms of moral weakness.[9]

5) "Social creativity is a minority function."[10] It is the moral *minority*, not the "Moral Majority," that most often makes a difference.

6) Jesus' call to a nonviolent transformation of society calls the church to an "evangelical non-conformity"[11] to the cultures in which we live. The prevailing pattern of civilization in our day as in Jesus' day is the use of violence and coercive power to achieve noble ends. Jesus offers another way. His church often does not.

The free-church offers this challenge to us today: there is a way to transform the world without ruling it. The church is called to be "salt" and "light," to be "leaven in the lump." When Christians are called to help govern, they do so first with a clear sense of the way of Jesus that is often counter to culture, and second with a modesty of purpose, that is, with the recognition that the state is not the realm of salvation. The kingdom of God heralded by the church seeks to transform the civic realm but is more than the civic realm.

FUNDAMENTALISM AND SECULARISM RECONSIDERED IN OUR POST-9/11 WORLD

T he "fundamentalisms" of our present age are the fearful and angry children of the modern age born in the previous century and gaining fullest strength in the current one. They are, therefore, quite young in the history of religions. Martin Marty in his summary volume *Fundamentalism Comprehended* describes the nature of the fundamentalisms of the three great monotheistic religions: Judaism, Christianity, and Islam:

> Fundamentalism, within these historic religious traditions, convinced of the conspiratorial nature of the secularists and liberal religionists, adopted a set of strategies for fighting back against what is perceived as a concerted effort of secular states or elements within them to push people of religious consciousness and conscience to be margins of society. [1]

Thirty years ago, in the 1970s, I could not have anticipated such a rise of fundamentalisms into the center of things. I could not have predicted the rise of power of right-wing religionists within the right-wing political resurgence in America. Nor could I have imagined the rise of fundamentalist Islamic terrorist groups onto the center of the world stage of politics and nations.

In her study of Christian, Jewish, and Islamic fundamentalisms in *The Battle for God*, Karen Armstrong describes the fundamentalist goal to "resacralize" society.[2] There is a wistfulness about this goal even nonfundamentalists can feel. The secular societies and secular nation states of the world have not issued into the "good society" with its dream of humankind come-of-age, emancipated from the shackles of religion now reaching an elevated form of human community.

What has ensued is a war of "worlds": a fundamentalist dream of a resacralized society, in which God's word and God's values are the law of the land, versus a secularist dream of a society freed from religious laws and the zealotry of religious passions. But resacralized societies threaten to recreate Europe's "wars of religion." As Blaise Pascal noted in *Pensées* in the seventeenth century, "Men never do evil so completely and so cheerfully as when they do it from religious conviction." At the same time secularist states have seen Stalin's murdered millions and Communism's ideological slaughterhouse.

Has the aggressive secularism of the modern age made much progress in the evolution of human society? Has the banishment of God from the public square exorcized the demons of violence, ignorance, and the abuse of power?

Armstrong says of the fundamentalists' goal:

> This battle for God was an attempt to fill the void at the heart of a society based on scientific rationalism.... Because it was so embattled, this campaign to resacralize society became aggressive and distorted. It lacked the compassion which all faiths have insisted is essential to the religious life and to any experience of the numinous.... But the fundamentalists did not have a monopoly on anger. Their movements had often evolved in a dialectical relationship with an aggressive secularism which showed scant respect for religion and its adherents. Secularists and fundamentalists sometimes seem trapped in an escalating spiral of hostility and resentment.[3]

42

This conflict seems to be fueling the culture-wars in America and the increased division between Democrat and Republican, liberal and conservative, and "red" and "blue" cultures.

Sometimes a temporary change in language can give us new eyes to see current patterns at work. I have been helped by a new set of categories Bruce Lincoln uses in his book *Holy Terrors: Thinking about Religion after September 11*. Instead of the more combative words "fundamentalist" and "secularist," he uses "maximalist" and "minimalist" to describe the two main positions on how religion and culture relate. [4]

A maximalist believes God's values should permeate the culture and be adopted by the state. Examples of maximalists include Sayyid Qutb, who has been called the "philosopher of Islamic terror," Jerry Falwell, founder of Moral Majority, and Martin Luther King Jr. A minimalist is someone who believes that religion should stay in its prescribed box on the edge of society and that its role in government and culture should be minimal. Examples of minimalism would include Thomas Jefferson, Tony Blair, and the American Civil Liberties Union.

Bruce Lincoln writes:

> One style—that of Qutb—I would characterize as maximalist, rather than "fundamentalist," a term that has inflammatory connotations and fails to capture what is really crucial: that is, the conviction that religion ought to permeate all aspects of social, indeed of human existence. The other, by contrast, is minimalist. This is the position taken by Kant at the culmination of the Enlightenment, which restricts religion to an important set of (chiefly metaphysical) concerns, protects its privileges against state intrusion, but restricts its activity and influence to this specialized sphere. [5]

A *minimalist* believes that religion has a sphere of influence in society but that it should have a minimal role in the public realm of law and politics.

A *maximalist* believes that God's laws and God's truth revealed in religion are indispensable for the health of society, so religious laws and values *must* become a part of a nation's political life.

You find *minimalists* in America, Israel, and Iraq, among Christians, Jews, and Muslims. Their roots are in the Enlightenment, in which, because of the incendiary uses of religion in war and civil strife, many concluded that religion should have a minimal role in public life and law. Our founders, notably Thomas Jefferson, were on the "minimalist side." Jefferson wrote in the Declaration of Independence, "We hold these truths to be self-evident, that all men are created equal." He carefully avoided the moral category of "revealed religion" and chose the broader category of "self-evident" moral truth. He wanted a society based on moral laws that were *self-evident* to all its citizens—of every religion and no religion—rather than on the revealed truth of particular religions. It was *not* self-evident to him at that time that slavery was wrong or that women should vote. That's just the point. A society should make its moral convictions as law only when they become self-evident to its citizens, not by edict of particular religion. Sometimes this takes time.

You also find *maximalists* in America, Israel, and Iraq. Maximalists are fearful that minimalism has moved us toward a secular godless society in which religious values are ignored and in which society has become morally decadent and self-destructive.

This is the view of the radical Islamic philosopher Qutb, who has influenced many extremist Islamic groups today. He spent time in America and was scandalized by its immorality by Islamic standards. He saw his nation, Egypt, becoming more and more secular. What he saw was what he called *jahiliyyah*, a culture of moral decadence. And the only way of defeating it was *jihad*, "holy struggle" externalized to become "holy war."

In America, conservative maximalists use the term "secular humanism," rather than *jahiliyyah*. They fear it has taken over our nation. So they see themselves as soldiers in a holy culture war to combat this secular humanistic culture. Their tactics are not violent, but they are incendiary, and they seek a political solution.

Of course, there are many places in the continuum between extreme *minimalists* on one side and extreme *maximalists* on the other, and there are multiple categories of both. Here are some:

Martin Luther King Jr. was a *maximalist* who believed God's values should be woven into the laws and hearts of a nation. His method was nonviolent resistance to unjust laws and unjust economic conditions. His values were the liberal values rooted in his black church tradition and in liberal Protestantism. Call him a *liberal maximalist*.

There are *conservative minimalists*, for example, "libertarians," who may want culture to exhibit spiritual values but who want government to exert minimal influence over the life of its citizens.

There are *religious minimalists* who want the separation of church and state for the sake of religious liberty. This has been a historic Baptist position. And there are *secular minimalists* who may be highly moral but don't see God as necessary for morality and don't want government in the morality business.

To push the categories further: There are *noncoercive maximalists* who want religious values spread voluntarily; and there are *coercive maximalists* who want them encoded legally.

Perhaps this reshuffling of categories can soften up the battle lines of our culture wars, provide some remedy for our advancing case of *categorical-sclerosis*, the hardening of the categories. So let us work toward a new language. It will help us discuss with less heat and more light what is at stake today: that ethical/moral/spiritual values should play a role in the public debate of what makes a good society or nation and that *how* these values play a role requires the most careful deliberation of its citizens.

At one point in our nation's history, it felt right that we be described as a "nation with the soul of a church."[6] But today we rightly say: *What* church? *Whose* church? And what about our citizens in synagogues, mosques, and temples, and those of no church? Do their moral values count? How should they count?

The twenty-first century is reexamining the categories of religion and politics. Secular democracies, religious theocracies, communist societies, and dictatorial autocracies are all thrown together in our global village. Religion will not go away, nor will political philosophies that want to restrain the influence of religion on government and society. This could be a contribution America makes in this century: a way to balance moral values and political freedom so to avoid both theocracy and an aggressively secular state. But only if we find new ways to talk with one another, the volume turned down across the divide of our current categories.

CHAPTER SIX

PUBLIC CHURCH IN AMERICA

If in the American tradition of "separation of church and state" the church is to be separate from the state, free to practice its faith, free from the encroachments of state power and free to challenge the state as its conscience leads, what is the proper role of the church in the public square?

Martin Marty has described its role as "the public church." He defines it this way:

> The public church is a family of apostolic churches with Jesus Christ at the center, churches which are especially sensitive to the *res publica,* the public order that surrounds and includes people of faith. [1]

The public church is made up of all three major strands of Christianity in America: Mainline Protestant, Evangelical, and Catholic, who determine that part of their calling is to enhance the common good. Their work is in the spirit of the prophet Jeremiah, who instructed the Hebrew people captive in Babylon: "Seek the welfare of the city where I have sent you into exile...for in its welfare you will find your welfare" (Jer. 29:7). The public church does not merely make forays into the public realm in order to save people in it but enters it for the sake of "the public as public." [2]

The public church does not give up the primary calling of its "saving faith," that is, its witness to the salvation it has been given and called to proclaim: reconciliation with God in Christ.

But it also sees itself called to practice "ordering faith," which "helps constitute civil, social, and political life from a theological point of view." [3]

Marty argues that "the public church" is different from the three main ways religions tend to organize themselves with regard to the public realm. The first he calls *totalist* in which the leaders seek to impose a complete set of norms on all the citizens. Examples are Chinese Maoism and Shi'ite Islam. This is the path of theocracy. It is what Bruce Lincoln names "maximalist" (see chapter 5).

The second path is *tribalist* in which religions become "fierce self-protective tribes" that protect and advance their religious identity. Marty gives these examples: Basques in Spain, the Gush Emunim in Israel, Protestants and Catholics in Northern Ireland, and militant fundamentalists in America.

The danger of tribalist religion is that its singular identity can turn into a "murderous identity." This is the phrase of Amin Maalouf, an Arab born in Lebanon now living in France, a "Melchite" Christian, and a novelist. When a group or person reduces its identity to one single affiliation, the world becomes a more dangerous place. What is different from 1992 when Marty wrote his book is that some of these tribes have gone global. Indeed, Maalouf describes ours as "the age of global tribes." [4] Al Qaeda is the militant vanguard of a tribalist form of Islam.

The third way religions relate to the public realm is *privatist*. Religion is seen as a private thing. This was the main solution modernism offered the world. Religion is individualistic, private, personal; it withdraws from the public square. This was the solution given our nation after the period of religious wars in Europe and defined by much Enlightenment thought. It is what Bruce Lincoln calls "minimalist." It is what most evangelicals in America were before they got politicized.

The problem with the privatist solution is that it left a vacuum for both political totalitarianism and fundamentalist totalism.

The public church offers another way beyond totalism, tribalism, and privatism. Its goal is *"to combine religious commitment with civility, spiritual passion with a public sense."* [5] As such public church contributes to what Benjamin Franklin in 1719 called "publick religion," which he saw as a "necessity" for the health of the republic.[6] Public religion is not the worship of the nation nor a political ideology becoming a religion. It is open theological conversation people carry on in the public square for the common good.

Martin Marty prefers the term "public religion" to Robert N. Bellah's famous term "civil religion." For as civil religion appropriates religious symbols for national self-identification, it can easily turn into a religiously backed nationalism, or into a worship of the civic realm as the final realm, what Will Campbell once termed "politics as Baal."[7] Moreover, "civil religion" tends to work from the top down, a kind of national religion, or religion of the nation, composed and controlled from the upper echelons of power. In his essay "An Anniversary to Forget," written for the *New York Times* the day after Hiroshima Day, August 7, 2005, Joicho Ito wrote of Japanese civil religion during World War II, that coming with the fall of the emperor, the Shinto religion also collapsed. The Shinto religion, Joicho Ito wrote, had been changed from decentralized animism into a state-sponsored war religion. So thus is religion co-opted to serve civil religion. In contrast, public religion is the voice, the many voices, of the people as they express their faith and theological convictions.

As religious people enter into public conversation about the common good, they bring the values and virtues of their faith. But they should also bring a quality of reverence that should temper the public debate. We are all seeking a truth that lies beyond us, ahead of us, a perfect truth found only in God. None of us possess it now. We can only be "one nation under God" when "under God" means that no one has the exclusive franchise on God.

"Public church" helps avoid the hazards of what Bill Moyers, following author Emilio Gentile, calls "political religion": religion used as "an instrument of political combat."[8] Political battles are seen in the eyes of the combatants as part of a larger cosmic battle. And we who fight assume, of course, that we are among the children of light and our opponents are among the children of darkness.

If religious people allow their religion to be used as an instrument of political combat, they undermine the public good they are trying to serve. This is not an easy line to walk. The

Republican party has recruited conservative evangelicals and conservative Catholics for its political cause, and the Democratic party has, somewhat more skittishly, recruited the help of progressive Christians and Jews. Religious folk new to the game find the lure of political power nigh irresistible.

The public church is wary of this danger, but it does not want to abandon the public square to secularists or fundamentalists—or to any one dominant religious group. James Madison liked to quote Voltaire that if a nation had one religion, it would characteristically persecute all others; if it had two religions, they would fight each other; and if it had many religions, they would find a way to get along. [9]

One of the dangers today is that religious people can be co-opted into becoming soldiers for a political religion of the Right or a political religion of the Left. The antidote is to let the many religious voices speak. As Martin Marty puts it, "A Republic prospers when many voices speak."

Toward this end, The Martin Marty Center at the University of Chicago has begun what it calls the "Public Religion Project." [10] Its purpose is to enhance the quality of religious discourse in the public square. Its work is: "To bring to light and interpret the forces of faith within a pluralistic society."

In its purpose to "bring to light" the voices of religion, it proceeds with this hope:

> "Bringing to light" means bringing entities into a zone where criticism can occur, mutuality can prosper, and no one can hide. When there are more voices at the table, it is likely that one may henceforth more likely enlarge the range of options for dealing with public problems and engage in celebrations for the renewing of public life.

The work of the Public Religion Project is a hopeful sign of the emergence of "public church" and "public religion" in America. Can religions enter the public realm without seeking to "draw the public into their zone of worship or claims for truth"? If so, religion can serve the common good and be health-giving rather than be destructive to the social fabric of the nation.

CHAPTER SEVEN

PRAYING WITH JESUS IN AN AGE OF "SACRED VIOLENCE"

When the hour of reality approaches, the zero hour . . . wholeheartedly welcome death for the sake of God. Always be remembering God. Either end your life while praying, seconds before the target, or make your last words: "There is no God but God, Muhammad is His messenger."
—Mohamed Atta, 9/11 terrorist leader

Here is America struck by God Almighty in one of its vital organs, so that its greatest buildings are destroyed. Grace and gratitude to God.
—Osama bin Laden

A commander-in-chief sends America's sons and daughters into a battle in a foreign land only after the greatest care and a lot of prayer. . . . May God continue to bless America.
—President George W. Bush

Neither party expected for the war, the magnitude, or the duration, which it has already attained. . . . Both read the same Bible, and pray to the same God; and each invokes His aid against the other. . . . The prayers of both could not be answered; that of neither has been answered fully. The Almighty has His own purposes.
—President Abraham Lincoln

Abba, forgive them; for they do not know what they are doing.
—Prayer of Jesus from the cross

C ould there be any time when we have needed more to
learn how Jesus prayed?

There is still in me the shock of seeing what my mind could
not comprehend: the two commercial airplanes flying into the
Twin Towers, then seeing the Towers collapse top floor to bottom
in minutes, with close to three thousand deaths resulting.

I was immediately grateful for the strong and decisive leadership of President Bush in the next days. And I was jarred by the
gloating of Osama bin Laden, al Qaeda's leader.

I found myself supporting some kind of swift action to bring
the terrorists to justice. It was one of the moments I found myself
resonating, perhaps too easily, with the words of Paul in Romans
13: "Let every person be subject to the governing authorities . . . For rulers are not a terror to good conduct but to evil conduct" (Rom. 13:1, 3). I thought of Martin Luther's distinction
between God's "right hand" at work in the redemption of the
world and God's "left hand" that maintains order and adminis-
ters justice.

Then came the speeches of the terrorists and the speeches of
American political and religious leaders that mingled religion
and war, prayer and violence. Here are some of them:[1]

First, the words of Mohamed Atta, leader of the terrorist group
in the 9/11 massacre. Left behind in his baggage, which didn't
make it onto the flight because of earlier delays (along with his
will and testament), his words were the final instructions written
for his group as they carried out their plans. He wrote:

> Pray the morning prayer in a group and ponder the great
> rewards of that prayer.

His instructions about the killing of airplane personnel during
the flights:

> If God decrees that any of you are to slaughter, dedicate the slaughter to your fathers and to _____.

The last word is unclear, but Atta's "God" is obviously involved in the transaction, for the word "dedicate" is a highly religious word. Violence as sacrament.

His last words are about the final moments of the mission:

> When the hour of reality approaches, the zero hour...whole-heartedly welcome death for the sake of God. Either end your life while praying...or make your last words: "There is no God but God, Muhammad is His messenger."

In President Bush's speech at the National Cathedral, September 14, 2001, in a memorial service for the slain, he said:

> But our responsibility to history is already clear: to answer these attacks and rid the world of evil.

On October 7, 2001, in an address to the nation, President Bush said:

> A commander-in-chief sends America's sons and daughters into battle in a foreign land only after greatest care and a lot of prayer. We ask them to leave their loved ones, to travel great distances, to risk injury, even to be prepared to make the ultimate sacrifice of their lives.

Osama bin Laden in a videotaped address on that same day, October 7, 2001, said:

> Here is America struck by God Almighty in one of its vital organs, so that its greatest buildings are destroyed. Grace and gratitude to God....As to America, I say to it and its people a few words: I swear to God that America will not live in peace before peace reigns in Palestine, and before all the army of infidels depart the land of Muhammad, peace be upon him. God is the greatest and glory be to Islam.

President Bush closed his October 7 speech with these words:

> The battle is now joined.... We will not waver. We will not
> tire, we will not falter, and we will not fail. Peace and freedom
> will prevail. Thank you. May God continue to bless America.

The Religious Right joined in with their own blessings of the
"war on terrorism" demonizing both terrorists and Islam. The first
name chosen for the U.S. military campaign included the word
"Crusade" before it was changed in fear of stoking religious
dimensions of the conflict. Then it was named "Operation
Infinite Justice," evoking more concern, then finally called
"Operation Enduring Freedom."

I began to feel a deep spiritual unease. At the same time, I
found myself praying the three prayers of Jesus from the cross.
They revealed something essential about Jesus and expressed
what I needed spiritually in those days after what could be called
an American crucifixion.

There is something essential about Jesus and about Christian
spirituality in these three prayers. They are: First, a prayer of
abandonment, *"Eli, Eli, lama sabachthani?"* That is, *"My God, my
God, why hast thou forsaken me?"* (Matt. 27:46 KJV). Second, a
prayer for forgiveness, *"Abba* (Father), forgive them; for they
know not what they do" (Luke 23:34 KJV). And third, a prayer of
relinquishment, *"Abba* (Father), into thy hands I commend my
spirit" (Luke 23:46 KJV). [2]

The prayer of abandonment. Perhaps we must always start here
when the worst has happened: the honest feeling raised to God
that we feel abandoned, even by God. There may be a deeper
trust we are trying to hang onto beneath the cry, but the cry is
still there.

Jesus lived in the most profound sense of God-belovedness all his
life. At his baptism he heard God's voice say: You are my son, the
beloved, in whom I am well pleased. He called God *Abba*, which
translates "Father," but which was an Aramaic word children and

adults used, a word intimate, trusting, affectionate—like our word "Dad" or "Poppa." In every one of the nine prayers Jesus prayed in the Gospels, he began with *Abba*. Except this one from the cross, the prayer of forsakenness. He was using the words of Psalm 22, the words he had memorized growing up, words the Hebrew people had prayed *in extremis* when they felt abandoned by God.

This is our cry when the darkest hour hits. We need God to protect us from the worst life can bring. But here we are, and the best God seems able to do is to protect us *in* the darkness, gird our hearts and minds, sustain our hope, but not protect *from* the darkness. And we pray that will be enough.

Unless we acknowledge the reality of what has happened, we cannot go forward.

The next cry is an astonishment, the prayer of forgiveness: "*Abba*, Father, forgive them; for they know not what they do" (KJV). When I reflected on this prayer of Jesus in morning worship a week or two after 9/11, a person in the congregation said to me: "Your use of that prayer makes me so mad. The terrorists *did* know what they were doing!" One does not move quickly or easily from Jesus' first prayer of forsakenness to this prayer of forgiveness.

Jesus' life and teaching brought a radical forgiveness. "Love your enemy," he said, "pray for those who harm you."

On the cross whom was Jesus forgiving, or asking God to forgive? (Sometimes we ask God to forgive someone before we are ready to do so.) Those closest to him who betrayed him? Yes. The collusion of Roman and Jewish leaders who found it expedient to put him away? Yes. The crowd who went mindlessly along? Yes. These and more.

This prayer forgives us all, for none of us knows the full extent of our sins or the extent of the harm we have done. Albert Speer, one of the leaders of the Third Reich, repented of his involvement in the Nazi regime. As part of the working out of his remorse and repentance he wrote his exposé, *Inside the Third Reich*. In a recent book, *Albert Speer: His Battle with the Truth*, the author suggests that for all his truth-telling, Speer was never able

55

to face the complete truth about how early it was that he learned about the Final Solution against the Jews. Was the reason for his incapacity that he—at some level—believed he could not admit the truth and live?

Jesus' bestowal of forgiveness reaches to us all. Can you hear the sound of Jesus' voice praying for you? It reaches to those places of culpability we acknowledge—and to those places we cannot face in ourselves.

Jesus' prayer on the cross was the beginning of a forgiveness movement that has reached around the world. Two thousand years later it is still healing the deepest wounds of humanity.

We see Jesus' forgiveness movement at work today. An example comes from the Civil Rights movement in America in the figure of John Lewis, one of the great young leaders of the Civil Rights movement, perhaps second only to Martin Luther King Jr. in stature, now a U.S. congressman from Georgia.

Lewis had been one of the leaders in the first Selma to Montgomery march. Governor George Wallace sent his troops to beat the marchers back, which they did with uncontrolled brutality. Lewis had his skull cracked open.

Years later, between terms as governor, Wallace, in a wheelchair, paralyzed by an attacker's bullet, called John Lewis and asked him to come visit. Lewis did.

Governor Wallace said, "John, I need your forgiveness. Can you find it in your heart to forgive me?" John said, "Yes, Governor, I forgive you." Then Wallace asked: "Do you think God has it in his heart to forgive me?" John replied, "Governor Wallace, I'm even more certain about that."[3] This is what is saving the world. And it starts with a prayer from the cross, a prayer that even now can form our lives.

The last prayer of Jesus was the prayer of relinquishment: "*Father*, into thy hands I commend my spirit" (KJV).

With this last prayer Jesus releases himself into the hands of God, whom he called *Abba*. Jesus is paraphrasing Psalm 31 in this prayer. Earlier in the Psalm the writer cries out:

In you, O LORD, I seek refuge;
Do not let me ever be put to shame...
I am the scorn of all my adversaries,
a horror to my neighbors...
I have become like a broken vessel. (Ps. 31:1, 11, 12)

In the midst of all this the psalmist says, "Into thy hand I commend my spirit." Into thy hand I commit my *ruach*, my breath, my spirit, my life. It is a phrase to live by and to die by: "O God, into thy hands I offer all I am and all I have and all I love."

It is the spiritual movement of "letting go." We say, "O God, I take my sticky fingers off the controls and place my life in better hands than mine." "O God," we pray, "I've done what I could. Finish this work. Into Thy hands."

I think that was the spirit of H. Richard Niebuhr when he objected (counter to his brother, Reinhold) to a prospective military intervention by the United States when Japan invaded Manchuria. His article was entitled "The Grace of Doing Nothing." Sometimes, he wrote, our *inaction* can be a witness to "the well-nigh obsolete faith that there is a God." God is at work in the deep processes of history. We need not jump in at every act of aggression and try to do God's work. [4] Does our willingness to go to war sometimes reveal a practical atheism? "Since God can't do anything, I suppose we must!"

There is the work God called us to do in this world. It includes the work of bringing to justice those who threaten the welfare of nations and peoples. But when does justice turn to vengeance? Why do Christians who follow the one who prayed these prayers go to war so easily and invoke God's blessing so quickly?

Wendell Berry writes:

> "Christian" war has always been a problem, best solved by avoiding any attempt to reconcile policies of national or imperial militarism with anything Christ said or did. The Christian gospel is a summons to peace, calling for justice beyond anger, mercy beyond justice, forgiveness beyond mercy, love beyond forgiveness. It would require a most agile interpreter to justify hatred and war by means of the Gospels, in which we are

bidden to love our enemies, bless those who curse us, do good to those who hate us, and pray for those who despise us and persecute us. [5]

There is, to use the thought of philosopher René Girard, a sacred violence near the heart of all cultures and all religions. We identify scapegoats and do violence to them in order to secure unity and preserve our way of life. All in the name of God.

What Jesus did on the cross was to expose the "mechanism of sacred violence" in all cultures that we may see it for what it is and do away with it. Flannery O'Connor wrote, "The man in the violent situation reveals those qualities least dispensable in his personality, those qualities which are all he will have to take into eternity with him." [6] In "the violent situation" of the cross, Jesus chose to be killed rather than to kill so that we could see into the darkness of the human heart and turn from it. I know no better place to start than by praying with Jesus those three prayers.

AMERICA'S PLACE IN THE WORLD

"Redeemer Nation" or "Leader Nation"?

In September 2002, the White House published the *National Security Strategy* (hereafter *NSS*).[1] My understanding is that such a document is prepared by the White House and National Security Council and is then given to the Defense Department and Joint Chiefs of Staff to implement as military strategy.

In his book *Citizenship Papers,* Wendell Berry judges that this document "if carried out would amount to a radical revision of the political character of our nation."[2] Jack Perry, former U.S. ambassador and professor of international studies at Davidson College, writes of his own misgivings about America's current foreign policy as articulated in the *NSS:* "I cannot help observing that if you are a believer in international law—if you are not a believer that 'Might makes Right' among nations—then this doctrine will send shivers up your back."[3]

As stated on page one, the strategic goal of the *NSS* is "to cre-ate a balance of power that favors human freedom." It is clear throughout, however, that this balance of power always means American military supremacy. The document speaks of the good of international alliances, but this good is dismissed if we feel the need to act unilaterally and preemptively. Here are some excerpts:

> While the United States will constantly strive to enlist the support of the international community we *will not hesitate* to act alone, if necessary, to exercise our right of self-defense by *acting preemptively* against such terrorists. (page 5, emphasis mine)

> Our forces will be strong enough to dissuade political adversaries from *pursuing* a military build-up in *hopes of surpassing, or equaling,* the power of the United States. (page 20, emphasis mine)

> The greater the threat, the greater the risk of inaction—and the more compelling the case for taking anticipatory action to defend ourselves, *even if uncertainty remains* as to the time and place of the enemy's attack. To forestall or prevent such hostile acts by our adversaries, the United States will, if necessary, act preemptively. (page 10, emphasis mine)

The NSS used as an epigraph for the head of part 3 a quotation from President Bush's speech at the National Cathedral, September 14, 2001, three days after 9/11: "But our responsibility to history is already clear: to answer these attacks and *rid the world of evil*" (emphasis mine).

To fight human evil may be an honorable purpose for a nation. It was our national purpose upon entering World War II. But "to rid the world of evil"? Such a purpose presumes God-like power, wisdom, and goodness. I do not wish to quibble over words but to ask, where has the NSS and such language led us since 2002?

It became the blueprint for invasion of Iraq and our war in Iraq. It became the blank-check funding of this war. It led President Bush to identify as evil not just the terrorists of 9/11 but anybody building "weapons of mass destruction" who is not friendly to the United States and to name Iraq, Iran, and North Korea as an "axis of evil."

There is explicit in this document that we will act unilaterally; that we can engage in preemptive war; that our geopolitical goal is not "the balance of power" as during the Cold War, but now the unchallenged superiority of American power; and that any military build-up by another nation that seeks to equal or surpass American power will be seen as a grave threat to our nation. U.S. Representative Robin Hayes said after his vote for the 2002 resolution to authorize the president to take action against Iraq: "The way to peace is through irresistible force."[4] If the Cold War doctrine was based on deterrent and "mutually assured destruction," the new doctrine is based on the unequalled power to destroy.

Jack Perry summarizes the "Bush Doctrine":

> It holds that American power is properly supreme in the world, and we must maintain its supremacy, by preemptive action if necessary; and that terrorism is the work of evil men who hate freedom and must be extirpated; and that without other authority we have the right to invade other countries we target and unseat their governments; and that all this is part of a "war on terrorism" which (apparently) will remain necessary until all evil terrorists and all evil regimes are eliminated.[5]

This present mood in America is what historian Arthur Schlesinger warns as the excesses of "messianism." We trust in our superior power and unassailable wisdom. Contrast the words of the *NSS* with the *Federalist Papers*, number 63 (written by James Madison), which said that our nation should heed the wisdom and judgments of other nations of the world as we deliberate upon our decisions. It gave two reasons:

> The one is, that . . . it should appear to other nations as the off-spring of a wise and honorable policy; the second is, that in doubtful cases, particularly when the national councils may be warped by some strong passion or momentary interest, the

61

presumed or known opinion of the impartial world may be the
best guide that can be followed. [6]

At times America has seen itself as an "elect nation" or
"redeemer nation" [7] with a special calling from God. Too often
this posture has led us to see ourselves as better than or different
from the other nations of earth. Perhaps we would best see ourselves rather as "leader nation," blessed by God with extraordinary
resources, power, influence, and knowledge, a nation that has
determined to use these gifts to make this world not perfect but
better, and to fight evil, not as the warrior of God who can rid the
world of evil but as one of God's servant nations called to lessen
evil's impact and thwart its worst designs.

Historians and political scientists may well argue the worthiness
of our present national direction and whether our present course
is or is not a radical departure from our past. What I offer here are
some theological judgments that are based upon biblical insights.

When a nation overreaches its calling as part of God's creation
and presumes to be God-like in its power, wisdom, and goodness,
the biblical word for this condition is "idolatry." And its speech
that claims such God-like authority is called "blasphemy."

Is our nation headed in this direction? It appears so to me, sor-
rowfully so, and the only remedy is the hard and patient work of
its citizens to right our path, for ours is a government "of the people, by the people, for the people," as President Lincoln so mem-
orably said.

Does such a judgment call President Bush or our current
national leadership "evil"? No. Such a charge would be itself an
act of hubris. It is to say that the temptation to want to have
God-like power, wisdom, and goodness is as old as Adam and Eve
and the serpent's temptation in the Garden. We must be at every
moment in every age vigilant of such temptation.

In Revelation 13 the Roman Empire is depicted as the "beast"
who claims God-like power, wisdom, and goodness and before
whom the world bows in false worship saying "Who is like the
Beast? Who can defeat it?"—a blasphemous perversion of the
psalmist's cry, "Who is like Yahweh? Who can compare with the

Lord?" Paul Tillich wrote that the claim of anything finite to be
infinite, or final in its own right, is demonic.[8] Such is the perennial
temptation of nations. It was Rome's downfall, and it is the downfall of every nation that overreaches, even if its goals and intentions are noble.

I offer one more biblical vignette. It is a comic little scene, but
most instructive. In Acts 14, Paul and Barnabas have gone into
Lystra and healed a man who was crippled. When the townspeople see the miracle they cry aloud: "The gods have come down to
us in human form" (Acts 14:11). And they called Barnabas *Zeus*
because he was the more impressive to look at and they called
Paul *Hermes* because he was the one who did most of the talking.

Now the local priest of the Zeus religion shows up bringing
oxen and flowers and makes a showy sacrifice at the feet of
Barnabas and Paul. What do they do? They tear their clothes, a
ritual act of horror in the face of such blasphemous adoration.
Then they say to the townspeople: "Why are you doing this? We
also are mortal with passions like you, and announce to you good
news, that you should turn from these vain things to a living
God..." (Acts 14:15). If Paul's words did not convince them, the
sight of these two in boxer shorts with knobby knees and varicose
veins did the trick.

Do we and our national leaders have the intellectual and spiritual
humility to see when our nation overreaches? In face of the genuflection of the world before our power and wealth, do we have
the moral capacity to tear our clothes?

If not, then it is up to a spiritually horrified citizenry who
senses something is wrong to tear the nation's robe and show our
human skinny legs. Thomas Jefferson defended the general education of the nation's citizens so that they could offer just critique
of their government. "For nothing" Jefferson wrote, "can keep it
right but their own vigilant and distrustful superintendence."[9]

THE POLITICS OF DOOMSDAY

Cosmic War and the Distortion Of Biblical Apocalyptic

> *There is no middle way for Americans: It is victory or holocaust. This book is a manual for victory.*
> —David Frum and Richard Perle, An End To Evil: How to Win the War on Terror

> *God has blessed a group of vanguard Muslims, the fore-front of Islam, to destroy America. . . . The wind of faith is blowing and the wind of change is blowing to remove evil from the Peninsula of Muhammad, peace be upon him.*
> —Osama bin Laden, videotaped address, October 7, 2001

> *But our responsibility to history is already clear: to answer these attacks and rid the world of evil.*
> —President George W. Bush, National Cathedral, September 14, 2001

> *There is an inbuilt nihilism in the more extreme forms of fundamentalism. Fundamentalists in all three faiths have cultivated fantasies of destruction and annihilation.*
> —Karen Armstrong, The Battle for God: A History of Fundamentalism

I have been struggling with this for some time: The misuse of Hebrew and Christian scriptures to justify the use of violence. War may be a tragic necessity at times in history. I do not know. Jesus, if I read him right, did not concede the point. But I want to say: *Not in God's name* do we choose violence; *not in God's name* do we go to war.

The reason I became a Christian was because of my experience of the love of Jesus as God's own love. When I grew up a bit, I realized this love was for everybody, not just me and my kind. The heart and cornerstone of Jesus' religion was the commandment inherited from his Hebrew faith: "Love the Lord your God with all your heart and mind and soul and strength; and love your neighbor as yourself." It is the heart of every true religion.

So why in *God's* name do we do violence to one another? Mark Juergensmeyer has studied religious violence in all religions at the turn of the twenty-first century and asks the poignant and crucial question:

> Why does religion seem to need violence, and violence religion, and why is a divine mandate for destruction accepted with such certainty by some believers?[1]

I proceed with the words of poet William Stafford in my ear:

> A poet, a person, a fallible human being, has to step carefully through a puzzling world.[2]

It is a puzzling world, and we have at times a puzzling Bible. I want to look at some of the most puzzling parts of the Bible: prophetic texts and apocalyptic texts.

There is a way of thinking in the Bible called *prophetic*: I call it the prophetic imagination. And there is a way of thinking called *apocalyptic*; I call it the apocalyptic imagination. These are terribly confused today in the popular phrase "biblical prophecy."

66

This confusion can lead to dangerous distortions of biblical truth. One of them is the notion of "cosmic war," in which we are conscripted into the army of the Lord to battle others in the army of Satan, and history becomes the final battleground. This is what I call "the politics of doomsday." We are marching not to Zion but to Armageddon.

It is the politics of the Muslim jihadist, of Timothy McVeigh, and of Eric Robert Rudolph, bomber of the women's clinics, the gay club, and Olympic Park. It is the politics of the dispensationalist preacher who gleefully announces that World War III began on 9/11, and "It's all in the Bible!" And it is the politics that tempts many in America today. It is so tempting to believe our nation is the army of the righteous fighting evil itself, forgetting the wisdom that in our human historical frame, there's something of the worst in the best of us, and something of the best in the worst of us. The Rapture theology of Tim LaHaye popularized in his *Left Behind* novels encourages such thinking. The *Left Behind* website once proclaimed: "The veil between the fiction of *Left Behind* and the reality of life today in the Middle East is a thin one."

Bill Moyers traces this kind of thinking in a recent essay in the *New York Review of Books* entitled "Welcome to Doomsday." The rather sardonic title is scarily apt because there is in this theology a perverse welcoming of the worst, a cheery prediction of a final cataclysm in which God will destroy the world in order to save it. As Moyers describes it: "A war with Islam in the Middle East is not something to be feared but welcomed—an essential conflagration on the road to redemption."[3]

It is as though the biblical story of Noah and the flood had never been told, with God's promise "never again" to send a flood to destroy the world. The sign of the promise was a rainbow: God took his warrior's bow, set it in the sky and strung it with all the colors of creation. God unilaterally and eternally disarmed. We might find a way to destroy God's world, but not God. In the mind of many today God has taken his bow from the sky and handed it to us to use in the final battle. This is the politics of doomsday. Onward Christian Soldiers. Barbara Rossing in her book *The Rapture Exposed*, characterizes Rapture theology with the phrase, "The world cannot be saved," and she cites Jewish theologian Yehezkel Landau, who says that such theology boils down to a perverse parody of John 3:16: "God so loved the world that he sent it World War III."[4]

As the expression goes, "Can we talk?" Most of what people call "biblical prophecy" today is neither "biblical" nor "prophecy" and is so far from the spirit of Jesus that this version of Christianity could be called, to use the words of Paul, "a different gospel" of "another Jesus" (2 Cor. 11:4).

What is called "biblical prophecy" today is the belief that the prophets in the Bible foretold faraway events that one day would come true because God has predetermined the course of history— including how, exactly, the world will end. I cannot imagine a much greater distortion of scripture.

Let me offer some clarifying definitions and distinctions between the prophetic and the apocalyptic in the Bible. I have been most helped by Harvard's Paul Hanson here.[5]

The prophets or *nebiim* of Hebrew scripture were those "called"—*nabi* means "one who is called"—to announce God's will and relay God's word to nations and peoples, primarily God's people called Israel. They had been given a vision of God's presence and God's will, and they applied it to "plain history, real politics, and human instrumentality,"[6] to use the words of Paul Hanson. So, for example, Isaiah is given a vision in the temple and is then commanded, "Go and say to this people..." (Isa. 6:9).

The prophet spoke believing that God's people might respond, repent, and turn, disaster might be averted and salvation be accomplished.[7] History was open-ended, not fixed. In the mind of the prophet, we were always, to use the words of a Texas cowboy poet, "just before beyond redemption."

Moses, who was regarded in Jewish tradition as *prophet* as well as lawgiver, speaks these words that are the heart of the prophetic message.

I have set before you life and death, blessings and curses. Choose life so that you and your descendants may live, loving the LORD your God, obeying him, and holding fast to him; for that means life to you. (Deut. 30:19-20)

We have a choice: shalom or chaos, life or death.

Now let's turn to the apocalyptic imagination. In popular usage "apocalypse" refers to a dark catastrophic period of history leading to death and the destruction of the world. We see this grim vision not just in religion and politics but in movies, literature, and music.

Apocalypse comes from the Greek noun *apocalypsis*, meaning "revelation" or "unveiling," and from the Greek verb *apocalypto*, meaning "to reveal, unveil, uncover." The book of Revelation (sometimes titled *The Apocalypse of John*) begins:

The revelation of Jesus Christ, which God gave him to show his servants what must soon take place; he made it known by sending his angel to his servant John. (Rev. 1:1)

The prophetic and the apocalyptic both have a person receiving a vision and delivering it to God's people. Here is Paul Hanson's distinction, which I find most helpful: The prophetic imagination applies the vision of God to "plain history, real politics, and human instrumentality." In contrast, the apocalyptic prophet lives in darker, direr circumstances. God's will cannot be worked out in "plain history, real politics, and human instrumentality." It is too late for that. God and God alone can redeem history by breaking into it from outside. The apocalyptic imagination sees a final cosmic battle between God and Satan, angels and demons. God will win the battle. *God* will bring the kingdom of God to earth; we will not. [8]

The apocalyptic vision is given to God's people, not to enlist them in the cosmic war, but to call them to stay faithful and not lose hope in the present dark days. So, for example, in contrast to Isaiah's call by God, we have in the apocalyptic vision of Daniel these words:

> But you, Daniel, keep the words secret and the book sealed
> until the time of the end. (Dan. 12:4)

The vision is for the righteous remnant, not for the world at large.

Apocalyptic literature is "crisis literature." It was born in post-exilic Judaism when the Hebrew people returned from Babylonian captivity only to be ruled by foreign rulers for centuries. We see it in the Dead Sea Scrolls of the Essene community. We see it in the time of Jesus during the Roman occupation. And we see it in early Christian literature as Christians were persecuted by Rome, e.g., the book of Revelation. [9]

What we should note, however, is the *commonality* of the prophetic and apocalyptic: both hope in a God who will not abandon the world or destroy it, but will remain faithful to it until the world is redeemed in a "glorified Zion" or in a "new heaven and new earth." [10] If you look at the last two chapters of Revelation, "the new heaven and new earth" is a transfigured earthly existence where the spiritual and the material are perfectly wed. The "New Jerusalem" comes from God as a bride adorned for her husband. There is an end of warfare, sickness, and death. There is even a "healing of the nations." Our hope is not just in heaven, but for earth. "Thy kingdom come, Thy will be done *on earth* as in heaven," Jesus taught us to pray.

If the world ends in catastrophe it will be what J. R. R. Tolkien called a "*eu*-catastrophe," a good catastrophe, an end that is cataclysmically good. To use the words of the mystic Julian of Norwich: "All will be well, and all will be well, and every kind of thing will be well." [11]

This leads me to three grave distortions of biblical apocalyptic today.

The first is literalizing the symbolic language of apocalyptic. To paraphrase theologian N. T. Wright in his book *The Millennium Myth*, this is like saying global warming caused the end of the Cold War. Apocalyptic literature is a highly coded symbolic language. Jesus is not literally a lamb; the thousand year-reign of Christ is not a thousand calendar years.

The second is catastrophizing the end. It is the belief that what God has planned for the world is its destruction so that a final realm of salvation can come. Much current "biblical prophecy" has a death-wish for God's world—which is just fine for the proponents of such theology because they will be saved or "raptured" out of it. It is not too strong for Karen Armstrong to say that such theology has an "inbuilt nihilism" and cultivates "fantasies of revenge" and "fantasies of annihilation." [12]

The third is historicizing cosmic war imagery and identifying our battles with God's cosmic battle. Our social conflicts are turned into holy war. There can be Christian jihadists as well as Muslim jihadists.

Mark Juergensmeyer says that religion does not ordinarily lead to violence, but it does so when there is a coalescence of "a peculiar set of circumstances—political, social and ideological—when religion becomes fused with violent expressions of social aspiration, personal pride, and movements for social change." [13] Religion then becomes an accelerant, a highly combustible agent added to stoke political and social fires, a theological justifier of deeper passions. It remains to be seen whether religion can be a healer, a de-accelerant of global passions, a de-justifier of our human violent ways.

The greatest danger comes when we link God's cosmic battle with our political and social struggles. As Juergensmeyer writes: "Conflicts in the real world are linked to an invisible, cosmic war: the spiritual struggle between order and disorder, light and darkness, faith and doubt.... It is when this cosmic war is confused with a struggle in the social world that religious violence becomes savagely real." [14]

We see the cultivation of the cosmic war way of thinking in the American "dispensational" preacher who links the war in Iraq with a coming Armageddon. We see it in Osama bin Laden's *fatwa* issued in 1998 that asserted that America's presence in the Middle East was "a clear declaration of war on God, His messenger, and Muslims." He said in his videotaped address, October 7, 2001:

God has blessed a group of vanguard Muslims, the forefront of Islam, to destroy America. May God bless them and allot them a supreme place in heaven. . . . The wind of faith is blowing and the wind of change is blowing to remove evil from the Peninsula of Muhammad, peace be upon him.

It is cultivated by David Frum and Richard Perle in their book, *An End to Evil: How to Win the War on Terror,* when they write:

There is no middle way for Americans: It is victory or holo-caust. [15]

It is cultivated in President Bush's words in the National Cathedral on September 14, 2001:

Our responsibility to history is clear: to answer these attacks and rid the world of evil.

It was cultivated in the name we gave to our military mission in Afghanistan: "Operation Infinite Justice." (How else could this be translated into Arabic but in the tone of holy war?) It was later changed to "Operation Enduring Freedom."

It was cultivated when in May of 2005, we saw this picture on the U.S. Marine website: a U.S. tank in Iraq with the words inscribed in large black letters across its gun barrel, NEW TESTAMENT, and the caption to the picture:

The New Testament . . . prepares to lead the way during a recent mission.

The picture was soon removed from the website.

How tragically wrong to use biblical apocalyptic imagery to sanction the use of violence. This can only happen by cutting it off from the larger biblical witness—and from Jesus.

In the book of Revelation, Jesus is pictured as the victorious Lamb, but he is also the suffering Lamb, his "wounds yet visible," reminding us that Jesus died for us and for his faith; he did not kill for us and for his faith. This is not Jesus as a wounded Rambo returning to wipe out his enemies and to enlist us in the battle.

The Lamb's way is still the way of the *Lamb*: nonviolent suffering love that stands as witness against the powers of evil in the world. And we followers of the Lamb are called not to violent battle for God but to steadfast faithfulness to the way of Christ, even in the face of persecution and death:

> If you are to be taken captive, into captivity you go; if you kill with the sword, with the sword you must be killed. Here is a call for the endurance and faith of the saints. (Rev. 13:10)

I cannot judge whether Muslim jihadhists today misuse the Koran and misappropriate the word *jihad* —which literally means "holy struggle." I suspect they do. But I can and do judge those Christians who use biblical apocalyptic literature to call Christians to violence and holy war. It is a false gospel of "another Jesus." In face of it, the shortest verse in the Bible may well apply: "Jesus wept" (John 11:35).

PART TWO

Preaching About Faith and Politics

The second half of this book is a compilation of sermons preached from 2002 to 2005 that deals with the issues raised earlier in the volume. There are also occasional pieces written for the public square. It may be helpful for the reader to see not only what I have said but also *how* I have said it at particular points in time. These pieces, therefore, have been only slightly edited from their original form. The oral form of these sermons occasionally omitted or summarized some of the longer quotations. They are presented here for the most part in chronological order, pages of a pastor's journey with a congregation in a time of falling towers, war, and a nation's search for itself.

CHAPTER TEN

CONVERSING WITH JESUS IN TIME OF WAR

I knew too that this new war was not even new but was only the old one come again. And what caused it? It was caused, I thought, by people failing to love one another, failing to love their enemies. I was glad enough that I had not become a preacher, and so would not have to go through a war pretending that Jesus had not told us to love our enemies.
—Wendell Berry, Jayber Crow

You have heard that it was said, "You shall love your neighbor and hate your enemy." But I say to you, Love your enemies and pray for those who persecute you, so that you may be children of your Father in heaven; for he makes his sun rise on the evil and on the good, and sends rain on the righteous and on the unrighteous. For if you love those who love you, what reward do you have? Do not even the tax collectors do the same? And if you greet only your brothers and sisters, what more are you doing than others? Do not even the Gentiles do the same? Be perfect, therefore, as your heavenly Father is perfect.
—Matthew 5:43-48

* This sermon, preached October 6, 2002, came during intense national debate on the looming war in Iraq and "just war" theories.

W e have been a nation at war since the terrorist attack on September 11, 2001. That war appears to be on the verge of expansion into a war with Iraq.

My heart is torn, my mind is overwhelmed by an avalanche of information, of conflicting opinions and of wrenching moral questions. I want to see all sides, but I cannot *take* all sides—though I desperately *want* to. (That is part of my neurosis.) The imminence of war has got me up at night these past weeks, and I've found myself writing scraps of sermons I might or might not preach. I dreamed last week that a local high school was destroyed by a bomb.

Preachers should not pose as experts in politics, foreign affairs, or military science. But we are called to bring the weight, the gravitas, of our spiritual tradition to bear on the most urgent issues of the day, including war and peace. Christian preachers are called in particular to help us talk seriously with Jesus as we wrestle with such questions. Jesus does not make it easy on us.

In Wendell Berry's novel *Jayber Crow*, Jayber, the main character, is the town barber for Port William, Kentucky. As a young man he felt called to be a preacher and enrolled as a pre-ministerial student at a small Baptist college—where he discovered he was not called to be a preacher.

Years later, as he lived through World War II with his friends and townspeople, he said "I was glad enough that I had not become a preacher, and so would not have to go through a war pretending that Jesus had not told us to love our enemies." [1]

Wartime places special stress on Christians. The apostle Paul wrote that we are citizens of two commonwealths, the commonwealth of our nation and the commonwealth of the kingdom of God. Sometimes dual citizenship brings us into agonizing inner conflict.

My purposes are two. First, to bring the resources of the Christian faith to bear on the war question. It is to give you tools with which to make up your own mind and form your own soul.

The second purpose is to help us reflect on what kind of church we want to be in a time when our nation will be divided on the war in Iraq, and when conscience will lead some to support the war and others to oppose it.

I think of a family during the Vietnam War. One of the sons entered the military and served in Vietnam. A second son became a conscientious objector to war and left the country in order to avoid the draft. The parents loved and blessed both sons. They created a home where the examination of conscience and the following of conscience were sacred responsibilities. The conscience should be *informed*, they believed, and it had to be *free* before God.

I would hope that our church could be such a place: where different stances on war would be passionately held and mutually honored. If the war expands, this will not be easy, and few churches will be such a place.

I am myself a Christian pacifist. I cannot as a follower of Jesus participate in combat, though I would go into combat as a chaplain or in another noncombatant role or perform some alternative service to my nation. Pacifism should not be used to excuse a person from service to one's nation or to protect oneself from the dangers others face. Conscientious objection to participation in war is a noble principle of American law. Few Christians let themselves seriously consider it.

I do not think one has to be a pacifist in order to be a Christian. I am moved by the story of Dietrich Bonhoeffer, the brilliant German theologian and Christian pacifist who relinquished his pacifism in order to join in a plot to overthrow the leader of his nation, Adolf Hitler. He was arrested and was executed by order of Hitler. He could not let his Christian pacifism remove him from his human responsibility as a German citizen.

The early church had a strongly pacifist stance in its first three hundred years. When Christianity became the official religion of the Roman Empire such a stance became increasingly complicated. What we call "just war" theory arose in the church to help guide Christians as they faced the moral dilemma of war. It was used to help Christians decide on a case-by-case basis whether they could join the military and be involved in war. And it became a way Christian leaders could speak to the "powers that be" and could work to restrain the violent measures of war.

"Just war" theory is not an exclusively Christian phenomenon. It is part of the repertoire of moral reasoning God has given to all humanity. In the century before Christ, the Roman philosopher and politician Cicero articulated principles of just war. My guess is that all cultures and religions have sought some form of moral limitation of war. If you read Hebrew scripture, guidelines were given to limit the insanity and fury of war. But there was also a dream, God's dream, that there would be a time when swords would be beaten into plowshares and spears into pruning hooks, and we would learn war no more.

There is today in our nation an intense moral debate going on about "just war" and our threatened invasion of Iraq. Let me offer in simplified form the main points of just war theory.

For a war to be just, it must meet these major criteria: One, there must be "just cause" (*jus ad bellum*) and two, there must be "just conduct" (*jus in bello*).

"Just cause" for war has generally meant:
1. It must be a war of self-defense; i.e., to defend against attack or immediate threat of attack.
2. It must have "competent authority," that is, be legally constituted by action of a nation and/or a league of nations.
3. It must be a "last resort," entered into only after all other measures have been exhausted.

"Just conduct" in war has, in general, included two main criteria:
1. The law of proportionality: the means of destruction must be proportional to the ends being sought. We must not become more evil than the evil we fight.
2. Protection against civilian and noncombatant deaths. There must be a low percentage of civilian casualties.

As you might expect, just war principles are being used today on *both* sides of the issue of war in Iraq. Human law is not perfectly delivered from heaven but hammered out in the messy, ambiguous, and difficult circumstances of history. As the nature of warfare changes, our application of law changes. And, I should add, the application of law is vulnerable to greater passions that may distort the original intention of the law.

We have an important and honorable debate going on in our nation. We do not carry on the debate well by pretending ourselves morally and intellectually superior and presuming our opponents wrongheaded or softheaded or morally inferior.

So let us enter the debate with clear heads and passionate hearts and respect for those who differ.

Where do I stand? Where do I stand today? With what I know, at this moment in time, *I cannot see invasion of Iraq as qualifying under just war principles.* Our president and our leaders, with what they know, will have to make their own moral decisions.

It seems we never know enough to make the hardest decisions of life. But as mortals we cannot wait for the moment of omniscience to make these decisions. We cannot expect from our leaders omniscience as they make decisions. They make, as we do, the best decisions they know to make. And having made them, none should presume infallibility.

But having said all that, I move more deeply—into conversation with Jesus, with his words and his life.

In the past, I have quoted the philosopher George Santayana, who said, "Every living and healthy religion has a marked idiosyncrasy. Its power consists in its special and surprising message and the bias which that revelation gives to life." [2]

What is the surprising and special character of the Christian revelation and the bias it brings to life in regard to the issues of war and peace? It is not in our advocacy of stringent just war criteria for war—as important as that is. Such advocacy is part of our mission as stewards of the moral tradition of humanity. But such is not our most unique and powerful witness as Christians.

Jesus was a faithful Jew who came saying that the law of Moses was the revelation of God, but that it was not the final and fullest revelation. He had the audacity to say: "You have heard it said of old [referring to the Mosaic law], but now I say to you." Such talk gets you killed.

Take the issue of divorce. In his day there was a conservative school that made divorce very difficult and a liberal school that made divorce much easier. But in both schools it was the man who had the power to divorce, not women. So one day Jesus was asked, How do you read the Torah on this? Are you a conservative or a liberal? Jesus said in effect: You argue over the law of Moses that was given by God because of the hardness of hearts— because of our unteachableness. If you want to know the true will of God, don't go back to Moses; go further back to creation, to the Garden, where God made Adam for Eve and Eve for Adam and said, "What God has joined, let no one put asunder."

He made a similar move on the question of war and violence.

> You have heard that it was said, "You shall love your neighbor and hate your enemy." But I say to you, Love your enemies and pray for those who persecute you, so that you may be children of your Father in heaven. (Matt. 5:43-45)

> You have heard that it was said, "An eye for an eye and a tooth for a tooth." But I say to you, Do not resist an evildoer. (Matt. 5:38-39)

"An eye for an eye and a tooth for a tooth" was a *restraining* of violence, a law of retributive justice that kept violence within limits—like "just war" theory. It said, if someone takes out your eye, you are not allowed to take *both* of theirs.

But Jesus pointed to a higher way, to the way of a "new creation" still straining to be born: the way of nonretaliation. It was not a popular word then—especially with the boot of the Roman oppressor everywhere on Jewish throats. Jesus did not presume everyone would follow. He predicted most would not. But it was the way he heard God command him to live, and he was going to live it out.

When he rode into Jerusalem on Palm Sunday he came riding not on a warrior's stallion but on a lowly donkey. He was redefining what "Messiah" meant, what "Anointed One" meant. He refused the path of violent revolution against Rome, however "just" it might have been. He wept over Jerusalem and said:

> If you, even you, had only recognized on this day the things that make for peace! But now, they are hidden from your eyes. (Luke 19:42)

Hold that image and place it next to the messianic vision of Isaiah in chapter 2: where all nations will flow to the mountain of the house of God and live in the light of God. God's holy hill will be a place where people will beat swords into plowshares and spears into pruning hooks, and we will learn war no more.

Look today at Jerusalem, the holy hill God hoped would reshape the world. It is divided Jewish, Christian, and Muslim, and all three religions are more than ready to beat their plow-shares into swords and their pruning hooks into spears. Today we see raised high the Christian sword, the Jewish sword, the Muslim sword. Do not think Muslim people can read America's military action as other than a Christian crusade. And America's conservative Christian spokespersons are making sure of it. Jerry Falwell's highly publicized remarks are but one illustration as he called Mohammed a terrorist.

So Jesus weeps still over that beloved and divided city and every city: Jerusalem, Baghdad, Washington, Beirut. Where can we find God's holy hill? Where can we flow and live in the light of God? Where will we learn war no more and find some higher way?

Jesus did not only say these words, he lived them. When he was arrested, he stopped his disciples from mounting a violent mission. There was no holy war in his heart. When a disciple cut off the ear of an arresting soldier, Jesus said, "Put your sword away. Those who live by the sword will die by it."

When examined by Pilate he said, "My kingdom is not of this world. If it were so, my disciples would be fighting." What he meant by "not of this world" was not the kingdom of God as an escape from the world into some spiritual realm, but that his kingdom would be deeply *in* the human historical world but not follow in its accustomed ways.

And when he died, he prayed, "Father, forgive them, for they know not what they do" (Luke 23:34). He died not with a sword in his hands but with a prayer for his enemies. *The one we follow as the Christ of God chose to die as a victim of violence rather than as a perpetrator of violence, however just.*

However we deal with the question of war and peace, we have to deal with Jesus, with his words and with his very specific way of death.

We may not be able to follow him—many days I cannot—and if we cannot, let us confess so; but let us not go through a war pretending Jesus didn't say, "Love your enemy."

Conclusion

How then do we live? How do we live together as a community of Christ? How can we be a people of differing conscience but not divided?

I think we do so as we become first and last a people of prayer. Not prayer as some kind of escape from action but as our daily breath that carries us on to live out our days with passionate conviction and deep humility. As a people who are trying to do justice and love mercy and walk humbly with God and one another.

So we kneel before the mystery of God and the terrors of life, in bafflement and moral anguish. We pray for our president and our nation's leaders and for the leaders of all nations and peoples. And we pray for our enemies, though our hearts recoil—how could they not recoil? We pray for Saddam Hussein and all who would do us harm. We pray for our soldiers and for the people of Iraq and Afghanistan and for a world that seems never to know the things that make for peace.

Amen.

CHAPTER ELEVEN

"IF YOU BEING EVIL"

War and the Providence of God

*Set the trumpet to your lips! One like a vulture is over
the house of the LORD, because they have broken my
covenant, and transgressed my law. Israel cries to me,
"My God, we—Israel—know you!" Israel has spurned
the good; the enemy shall pursue him. They made kings,
but not through me; they set up princes, but without my
knowledge. With their silver and gold they made idols for
their own destruction. —Hosea 8:1-4*

*As he rode along, people kept spreading their cloaks on the
road. As he was now approaching the path down from the
Mount of Olives, the whole multitude of the disciples
began to praise God joyfully with a loud voice for all the
deeds of power that they had seen, saying, "Blessed is the
king who comes in the name of the Lord! Peace in heaven,
and glory in the highest heaven!" Some of the Pharisees in
the crowd said to him, "Teacher, order your disciples to
stop." He answered, "I tell you, if these were silent, the
stones would shout out." As he came near and saw the
city, he wept over it, saying, "If you, even you, had only
recognized on this day the things that make for peace! But
now they are hidden from your eyes." — Luke 19:36-42*

*This sermon was preached on March 23, 2003, the week our nation launched
the war in Iraq.

I have not ever wanted less to be up here in the pulpit. We are at war. Perhaps we have been since the Twin Towers fell. The world seems changed since 9/11, at least our world, bewilderingly and breathtakingly so. People-groups as well as nation-states wage war. And God's name has reentered the vocabulary of war.

James Forbes, senior minister of Riverside Church in New York City, remarked this week that war breaks all ten of the Commandments. Not the least of which is the third: "Thou shalt not take the name of the Lord thy God in vain."

If war does break all ten, it is right then that no matter how "just" we may feel the present war to be, we sing our *Agnus Dei*:

> O Lamb of God,
> that takest away the sins of the world,
> have mercy on us.

Friday I went rummaging through my study cabinets looking for an old notebook. I came upon an old photograph, six or seven years old, of me shaking hands with then Texas Governor, now President George Bush. It was at an educational summit that my church in Fort Worth, Texas, was hosting. In the picture we are smiling, both looking younger, relatively carefree, years before these unimaginable times.

Seeing the picture called me to another round of prayer: for President Bush, for our nation, for our world. In my prayers I do not tell God what to tell President Bush. I hate it when people pray that way for me—so sure of what God ought to be doing in my life.

But I prayed. And now I preach. One of my rules for preaching is that whomever I mention in sermons, I speak as if that person were in the same room. It is a way of keeping my language "I/Thou" language rather than "I/It" language, that is, talking to a sacred other rather than talking about them, reducing them to an "it," an object. It would be a good rule for all speech.

So I proceed.

The times: How can one read "God" in them? How can we live with some measure of hope in them? To ask the "God" question—Where is God? What is God doing in this?—is to search for some intelligibility about life; it is to seek a basis for hope.

The difficulty of moral clarity in the present darkness was underscored the other day when the *Charlotte Observer* published two essays, one by former President Jimmy Carter and the other by Elie Wiesel, Auschwitz survivor, writer, and Nobel Peace Prize recipient. Here were two of my moral heroes, and they took opposite positions on the war: Carter against the war with Iraq, and Wiesel for it. In Jimmy Carter's Nobel Peace Prize lecture on December 10, 2002, he said:

> War may sometimes be a necessary evil. But no matter how necessary, it is always an evil, never a good. We will not learn how to live together in peace by killing each other's children.

Today's sermon is my second one seeking some light and truth on the war question from a Christian perspective. The first was last October: "Conversing with Jesus in Time of War." This sermon follows from it.

It is as far as I can see in the present darkness. I don't presume to see very far. Perhaps we can see farther together. Perhaps God will help us see.

I begin with Jesus' phrase, "If you then, who are evil." It is a rather uncomfortable phrase, implying as it does that evil can be in us. Here's the whole sentence:

> If you then, who are evil, know how to give good gifts to your children, how much more will your Father in heaven give good things to those who ask him! (Matt. 7:11)

Later he would say:

> For out of the heart come evil intentions, murder, adultery, fornication, theft, false witness, slander. (Matt. 15:19)

The Ten Commandments are first broken inside us.

I do not think Jesus was saying that we by nature *are* evil. There is an essential goodness to us. God created us; in God's own image God made us, then blessed us and called us good. Jesus was reflecting the deep moral wisdom of his people: that each of us is capable of good and evil. To use Hebrew phrases, there is within each of us a *yetzer hatov*, a good impulse, *and yetzer hara*, an evil impulse.

Which will win our hearts? There's a story of an Alaskan Eskimo who had two dogs, one white, the other black. He trained them to fight one another for betting sport. Every Saturday he took them to town where people would wager on which would win. Some days the black dog won; other days the white dog won. But the Alaskan owner always won. He was asked, "How do you know which one is going to win?" He replied, "The one who wins is the one I feed during the week." Which do you feed? The *yetzer hara* or the *yetzer hatov*? Sometimes we don't, at the time, know which we are feeding.

I begin here to underline the moral ambiguity of human life, especially the moral ambiguity of human power. We are all capable of evil, and we all live with some admixture of good and evil. The word "evil" has been all too frequent a word in our political vocabulary since 9/11. Our political and religious leaders have used it against other nations and religions. And others have used it against us.

The danger of such language is that it makes of our causes "holy causes" and of our wars "holy wars." The danger is in what some call "moral splitting": we assign to others absolute evil and to ourselves perfect good. But this moral splitting denies the deeper biblical truth: we at every point are capable of both good and evil.

In discernment of good and evil, one cannot always depend upon the disposition of one's heart. As Jeremiah said, using words as uncomfortable as Jesus' words,

> The heart is devious above all else; it is perverse—who can understand it? (Jer. 17:9 KJV)

And neither can we depend upon our sincerity or the goodness of our intentions. As philosopher Susan Neiman writes:

> What counts is not what your road is paved with, but whether it leads to hell. [1]

So we begin there: With a moral caution and the recognition of the mixture of good and evil in all of us.

As I pondered scripture, the text from Hosea the prophet came vividly forth. It is a divine challenge to us and to every nation on earth.

Hosea saw his nation Israel threatened by the superpower Assyria, and he saw his nation headed toward disaster, not so much by Assyria's hand as by its own hand. Chapter 8 begins: "One like a vulture is over the house of the LORD." Hosea was speaking of his own nation. The reasons? "They have broken my covenant and transgressed my *Torah*."

The nation says to God: "My God, we—Israel—know you."

But God demurs: "They have spurned what is good.... They made kings, but not through me....With their silver and gold they made idols for their own destruction." (Our idols today are not made of silver and gold; our idols *are* silver and gold.)

Thus says Yahweh: "They sow the wind, and they shall reap the whirlwind...." Though they bargain with the nations ... they shall soon writhe under the burden of kings and princes" (Hos. 8:1-10).

It is a picture of a nation that has lost its way. The images are disquieting. They cut to the heart. They ask questions of our nation today and every nation.

These words picture what scripture calls "the judgment of God." The judgment of God is not God's petulant punishing of our misdeeds. Judgment is the human outworking of our sins, of our injustice and violence and unrighteousness. Judgment is the pain we experience as a result of our own deeds that can bring us—if we let it—to repentance and healing. We can finally hear what we must hear if we are to live: "You must change your life."

For judgment is never God's last word; it is the prelude to God's mercy. Hosea would then later offer this word. In face of Israel's defection from God's way, God says:

> How can I give you up, O Ephraim? How can I hand you over, O Israel?...My heart recoils within me; my compassion grows warm and tender. I will not execute my fierce anger...for I am God, and no mortal, the Holy One in your midst, and I will not come in wrath. (Hos. 11:8-9)

What is God doing in these times? Can we speak meaningfully of "the Providence of God"? I do not think we can speak of the Providence of God as protection of the innocent from death. In any war, it is the innocent who suffer most.

I think we can speak of the Providence of God as spiritual strength and comfort to those trying to do the good. We can speak of the Providence of God as the God who watches over your well-being and at the same time watches over every person's well-being and at the same time watches over the whole world, loving it with infinite patience and love toward redemption.

We dare not speak too glibly: six million Jews slaughtered in the *Shoah*; 240,000 people killed in Hiroshima; close to 3,000 lost on 9/11.

But to live with hope is to believe, to "faith," that God is moving creation toward justice, love, and peace—and that, whether or not *we* are on the side of justice, love, and peace.

There is a mercy beyond every judgment.

When I was in seminary, among the pantheon of theological gods were the Niebuhr brothers, H. Richard and Reinhold. We were taught to love our "Niebuhrs" as ourselves. In 1931 they had their first and only public argument. It was over whether the

United States should intervene militarily when in September, 1931, Japan invaded Manchuria.

H. Richard Niebuhr wrote an article entitled "The Grace of Doing Nothing," arguing for nonintervention. Sometimes *inaction* can be a witness to "the well-nigh obsolete faith that there is a God." God is at work in the deep processes of history. We need not feel we must jump in at every instance of aggression and do God's work.

Reinhold answered back in his article "Must We Do Nothing?" He accused his brother of a moral perfectionism, which would keep us from ever intervening in the face of human evil or injustice. [2]

The same debate rages on today: How should we oppose human evil?

A decade or so later, H. Richard reflected more deeply on war from the midst of World War II. He offers two images, which I pass on to you.

The first is "War as the Judgment of God." [3] To speak of war as God's judgment is to focus on what God is doing rather than on what we are doing. In war there is justice at work, though in better Hands than ours—and often hidden from our sight. In war, the judgment of God is at work, God acting in human suffering to bring people and nations to repentance, healing, and wholeness. War then is not *hell*—for in hell, God is absent. War is *purgatory*: God with us, moving us through pain and suffering to purification and redemption.

To speak of "War as the Judgment of God" is to put aside our passing of judgments on others and to ask, "What is *my* duty?" We can preoccupy ourselves with the passing of judgments—who is right and who is wrong—whether those judgments are aimed primarily at Saddam, or the United Nations, or President Bush, or Democrats, or war protesters, or war supporters.

But our first occupation should be the question of what *our* duty is. What does your duty require of you? Your duty as a follower of Jesus, as an American, as a citizen of God's world? Your duty to God, to nation, to creation, to neighbor, and to the world of neighbors?

You are called to forge in the "smithy of your soul," in the crucible of your conscience, your highest duty. And then act upon it!

President Bush is fulfilling to the best of his abilities his sworn duty to protect this nation. I will continue to pray for him the wisdom and inner strength to meet the extraordinary challenges of this day.

It is your duty and mine to act as our conscience leads. The glory of democracy is that the "good" is not handed down directly from God through the king to the people, but rather is hammered out in the messy, loud, sometimes contentious processes of debate and discernment.

And the determination of one's duty is not a position taken once but is an ongoing journey as life unfolds and the war proceeds. Before a war begins we ponder the issue of *jus ad bellum*—just cause for war. During a war, we wrestle with *jus in bello*—just conduct of war, a terrible but necessary moral calculus. And at the end of war we grapple with the *just conclusion* of war and the *just repair* of the world, in all the ways the world needs repair after war.

Let us keep the moral conversation going.

H. Richard gives us one more image, which I can only briefly develop: "War as Crucifixion."[4] In war, as in the crucifixion of Jesus, there were the innocent and the guilty among those crucified, and the innocent and the guilty among the crucifiers. And God is acting to save them all, us all.

In war there is a great savagery, and in war there is a great sacrifice: the sacrifice of young men and women for their ideals and for their country. And the sacrifice of their parents and their families.

Can we believe in a God who saves through crucifixion? Who hates war but who works in the midst of slaughter and sacrifice, heroism and cruelty to move this human race to some higher plane?

Such a faith does not remove from us the responsibility of agonizing moral choice in a dangerous world. But it does teach us to act with the spiritual mixture of conviction and humility. And it saves us from, on the one hand, the arrogance of moral certainty and, on the other, the swamp of moral relativism.

I know no greater example of this spirit than Abraham Lincoln during the American Civil War. However naturally profound he may have been, the agony of presiding over a civil war drove him to even deeper places of truth and faith. He did not call America "God's chosen nation"—as politicians and preachers loved to do then as now—but rather "an almost chosen people." Might does not make right. In an address in New York in 1860, he stated:

> Let us have faith that *right makes might,* and in that faith, let us to the end dare to do our duty as we *understand* it. (Emphasis mine.)

His Second Inaugural Address, delivered four years into the war, displayed a profound mixture of conviction and humility which could only come from a man of deep faith who had led a nation through the horrors of civil war. In God's eyes, in God's heart, is not every war a civil war? Lincoln's words give us a way to hold in our hearts this day the good of our nation, the good of the Iraqi people, and the good of the world:

> Neither party expected for the war the magnitude or the duration which it has already attained.... Each looked for an easier triumph, and a result less fundamental and astounding. Both read the same Bible and pray to the same God, and each invokes His aid against the other.... The prayers of both could not be answered. That of neither has been answered fully. *The Almighty has His own purposes.* (Emphasis mine.)

Lincoln could not calculate all the "costs" of the war, but he bowed beneath the judgments of God, judgments he described, quoting scripture, as "true and righteous altogether," judgments which would come to both sides of the conflict.

And he ended the speech with unforgettable words, words which kindle our best faith, hope, and action on behalf of our nation and world this day:

> With malice toward none; with charity for all; with firmness in the right, *as God gives us to see the right,* let us strive on to finish the work we are in ... to do all which may achieve and cherish

a just, and lasting peace, among ourselves, and with all nations. (Emphasis mine.)

Conclusion

What would Jesus do? The question is more than a bracelet we wear. I do not think he would be bearing arms into battle. He refused such choices in his day—and under similar pressures as in our day. He would probably have in his company of disciples both those for the war and those against it. He had that kind of mix in his own group of disciples. He would, no doubt, be weeping as he wept over Jerusalem, saying:

> If you, even you, had only recognized on this day the things that make for peace! (Luke 19:42)

Weeping over every city and nation, Washington and Baghdad, Jerusalem and Beirut, Paris and London, Belfast and Monrovia.

And I think he would be crying out these words from God as did Hosea:

> How can I give you up, O America!
> How can I let you go, O Iraq!
> My heart recoils within me;
> My compassion grows warm and tender.
> I will not execute *jihad*,
> I will not bring "shock and awe,"
>   for I am God, not human,
> The Holy One in your midst,
> and I will not come to destroy.

CHAPTER TWELVE

THE DEATH OF JESUS, WHICH IS LIFE TO THE WORLD

"Yes'm," The Misfit said . . . "Jesus thrown everything off balance."
—Flannery O'Connor, "A Good Man Is Hard to Find"

I want to speak to you this opening morning of Holy Week about the death of Jesus, which is life to the world.

We can no longer see the planet Earth the same way once we have seen a photograph of Earth taken from the moon: one blue-green jeweled sphere.

Neither can we see the world the same way since the cross of Christ. It is planted in the earth, but it reaches to heaven. When we see its form, backlit by the shining light of the love of God, everything is changed. It was what John the Baptist saw way back at the Jordan: "Here is the Lamb of God who takes away the sin of the world!" (John 1:29). To begin to fathom this is to begin to feel what God intends for us all: wholeness. Wholeness from the inside out and in the processes of history itself.

*This sermon was preached on April 13, 2003, Palm/Passion Sunday, the beginning of the Christian Holy Week, about one month into the war in Iraq.

The cross of Christ reveals the truth hidden from the foundation of the world, the truth about us, and the truth about God.

What is this truth? We start here. That human culture and the human psyche are bound up in the mechanism of "sacred violence."[1]

It is the violence done in the name of God or in the name of our highest allegiance, whatever that highest allegiance is. Roger Williams named some of these allegiances: God—Belly, God—Land, God—Nation. Scapegoats are found, then cast out or killed in order to maintain our unity, our order, our innocence, our purity and values.

It happens as we project our inner shadow on others; it happens as we triangulate in relationships and form a bond with one by disparaging another. It happens in schoolyards and in hallways, in boardrooms and war rooms, in city halls and sanctuaries and palaces.

Jesus went to his death to unmask the mechanism of sacred violence in the human heart and in society. He died at its hands in order to expose it and bring about its eventual abolition.

The whole Bible has been trying to reveal this truth, trying to tell the story, trying to separate the god of sacred violence—which is the creation of human culture—from the true God of the Bible: the Creator and Lover of the world, a God of endless love and healing forgiveness, a God "pruned of violence."

The Bible on my desk at home has 1,146 pages. On page 4 is the first murder. Cain kills his own brother. The murder is committed out of a fatal confusion about the kind of sacrifice God wants. Abel's blood cries out from the earth, and God says to Cain: "What have you done?"

Tragically near the heart of all three Abrahamic religions—Judaism, Christianity, and Islam—is the impulse of sacred violence: the violence of the zealot, the crusader, the jihadist. It is the violence of the Christian Crusades and the Spanish Inquisition, of Salem witch-hunts, and of lynchings in the South. Forgive me for bringing up this terrible chapter in our region's history. It has been documented: Sundays were the preferred days for lynchings, ministers were almost always there, and Christian hymns were sung, like "Onward Christian Soldiers" and "The Old Rugged Cross." It was a ritual of human sacrifice done in the name of God and holy culture.

Sacred violence is the violence of suicide bombers; it is the twisted logic of the twisted cross and the Holocaust; it is the passion of hate crimes. It is the holy zeal of any nation that drives a war past the rule of law and the protection of innocent life. It is what makes of our causes "holy" causes.

But Jesus, to quote The Misfit in Flannery O'Connor's story "A Good Man Is Hard to Find," "Jesus thrown everything off balance." [2]

Paul Johnson, the historian, frames the question:

> By the time of his trial and passion Jesus had succeeded in uniting an improbable, indeed unprecedented coalition against him: The Roman authorities, the Sadducees, the Pharisees, even Herod Antipas. And in destroying him, this unnatural combination appears to have acted with a great measure of popular support. What conclusions can we draw from this? [3]

I draw this: the crowds were in on it. Democracy was in on it. The Jewish leaders were in on it. The conservatives and the liberals were in on it. The Bible scholars were in on it. The bureaucrats were in on it. The great Roman Imperium was in on it, killing a few more that day in the name of the *Pax Romana*, the famous Roman Peace. The best and the brightest were in on it. The most religious and spiritual were in on it. The narcotic of war was in on it; the spiritual frenzy of inquisition and blood sacrifice was in on it.

Were you there when they crucified my Lord? Yes, I was there. We all were there: voting, jeering, silent, enthralled, confused, tortured, hoping that maybe with this man's death things might be better now. We were all there.

The myth of sacred violence was voiced by Caiaphas, the high priest:

> You do not understand that it is better for you to have one man die for the people than to have the whole nation destroyed. (John 11:50)

It is our human way: we channel our violence toward expend-able victims in the hope that their banishment or death may be the saving of the whole. This is the myth Jesus unmasked and exposed for what it is, a lie.

Jesus speaks of this lie when he says in John:

> Indeed, an hour is coming when those who kill you will think that by doing so they are offering worship to God. And they will do this because they have not known the Father or me. (John 16:2-3)

We think we can save ourselves at the expense of another. But this is a lie; it is not the truth. This is what Jesus revealed on the cross, and this is why his death is life to us.

The message is what God has been trying to say to us from the first pages of scripture, though sometimes it is hard to find, there in that ocean of words. It is the God trying to be revealed when the angel stopped Abraham's hand from sacrificing his son Isaac and supplied instead a ram.

It is the God the prophets tried to reveal when they said: "I want mercy, not sacrifice," says the Lord.

It is the God revealed in the great prophetic summary of Micah:

> "With what shall I come before the LORD, and bow myself before God on high? Shall I come before him with burnt offer-ings, with calves a year old? Will the LORD be pleased with thousands of rams, with tens of thousands of rivers of oil? Shall I give my firstborn for my transgression, the fruit of my body for the sin of my soul?" He has told you, O mortal, what is good; and what does the LORD require of you but to do justice, and to love kindness, and to walk humbly with your God? (Mic. 6:6-8)

This is the God that Jesus lived and died to reveal.

Jesus willingly, consciously threw himself against the wheel of the violent sacred so as to expose it and stop its historical path of destruction. He did so to unmask it and reveal it for what it is, a lie: *It is not of God; it will not save.*

Of his coming death Jesus said:

> The hour has come for the Son of Man to be glorified. Very truly, I tell you, unless a grain of wheat falls into the earth and dies, it remains just a single grain; but if it dies, it bears much fruit....Now is the judgment of this world; now the ruler of this world will be driven out. And I, when I am lifted up from the earth, will draw all people to myself. (John 12:23-24, 31-32)

The cross of Jesus is the judgment of the world, the unmasking of the mechanism of sacred violence near our hearts and near the heart of all religion and all culture. "Yes'm," The Misfit said, "Jesus thrown everything off balance."

Since the death of Jesus, every victim's face is the face of Jesus. Since the cross, every victim's face is our face.

But the truth we see at the cross would not be a saving truth were it not also a truth about *God.* I have taken too long to get here, but I'm now here.

This is a God who leaves the ninety-nine sheep safely in and goes after the one who is lost. God cares for the one excluded, the outcast, the "other," the one who is different. This is the gospel that almost got Jesus killed in the first sermon in his hometown—and eventually got him killed in Jerusalem on a Roman gallows.

God is the God who loves us all, righteous and unrighteous, just and unjust, thugs and murderers, law abiders and outlaws, graced and disgraced. There is no longer an inside and an out. Not with God. Not with God's people.

Do you remember Jesus' word from the cross? It is an unimaginable word: "Father, forgive them, for they know not what they do." None of us ever knows the full harm we do, or why we do it. But God forgives us.

This is the Easter light dawning behind the cross for all the world to see. It is the love of God that is drawing all people to God's self in Christ.

Here we are, here we *each* are: both lover and killer, perpetrator and victim, harmed harmers all; here we are, kind and cruel, faithful and faithless. And God loves you all. God loves every atom of you.

We were *all* there when they crucified our Lord. And we were all forgiven there!

And now we are all invited to the banquet of the kingdom where *all are welcome* and *all is reconciled*.

Stephen caught sight of this kingdom while being stoned to death. He prayed aloud: "Lord, do not hold this sin against them" (Acts 7:60).

Saint Thomas More got the truth. As he was led to execution and the executioner's block drew near, he expressed the desire that he and his executioner "be jocund together"—joined together in mirth—"at the heavenly banquet."

Martin Luther King Jr. caught the vision. He had seen the cross and he had glimpsed the promised land. The movement he led, a nonviolent opposition to injustice and racism and war, caught the character of Jesus' kingdom of God: the *means* had to be consistent with the *ends*, the opposite of the logic of sacred violence. Dr. King said:

> Returning violence for violence multiplies violence, adding deeper darkness to a night already devoid of stars. Darkness cannot drive out darkness; only light can do that. Hate cannot drive out hate; only love can do that. [4]

A couple of months before his assassination, King, preaching at Ebenezer Baptist Church, talked aloud about what he would want said at his funeral. "Tell them not to mention that I have a Nobel Peace Prize . . . Tell them not to mention that I have three or four hundred other awards, . . ." he said. "I'd like somebody to mention that day, that Martin Luther King, Jr., tried to give his life serving others. I'd like for somebody to say that day that Martin Luther King, Jr., tried to love somebody. I want you to say that day, that I tried to be right on the war question. I want you to be able to say that day that I did try to feed the hungry. . . . Yes, if you want to say that I was a drum major, say that I was a drum major for justice; say that I was a drum major for peace . . . And all of the other shallow things will not matter. I won't have any money to leave behind. I won't have the fine and luxurious things of life to leave behind. But I just want to leave a committed life behind." [5]

He had seen the cross, Jesus' death, which is life to us. He had heard the words, "Father forgive." He had seen Easter light dawning behind that dark cross.

And you?

CHAPTER THIRTEEN

GROUND ZERO SPIRITUALITY

From Jerusalem to Lisbon to 9/11
Texts Isa. 62:10-12; Luke 21:20-28

> *The eighteenth century used the word Lisbon much as we use the word Auschwitz today. . . .The 1755 earthquake that destroyed the city of Lisbon . . . shook the Enlightenment all the way to East Prussia, where an unknown minor scholar named Immanuel Kant wrote three essays on the nature of earthquakes for the Konigsberg newspaper. He was not alone. . .Voltaire and Rousseau found another reason to quarrel over it . . . and the six-year old Goethe, according to several sources, was brought to doubt and consciousness for the first time.*
> —Susan Neiman, Evil in Modern Thought

W hat do we do, how do we think, how then do we live when the unthinkable happens? There are events in history, in our lives, which are a "shaking of the foundations." Poet Robert Nathan's words become ours, "Now from the world the light of God is gone."[1]

---

*This sermon, preached December 7, 2003, pondered the meaning of living in catastrophic times.

Three such events were the destruction of Jerusalem by Rome in 70 C.E., the destruction of Lisbon by earthquake in 1755, and the destruction of the Trade Towers in New York City, September 11, 2001.

It is difficult for us to imagine the horror of Jerusalem's destruction in 70 C.E. Jesus had prophesied that it would happen—no stone left unturned, even God's temple destroyed—and so it happened. The "powers that be" thought that by executing him the disaster would be averted. It was not.

The Jewish historian Josephus reported that in the Roman siege of Jerusalem one million Jews were slain—and ninety-seven thousand were taken captive. Both Jewish and Christian faiths were shaken to their roots.

How does one make sense of something like this? The Jewish Josephus, using the theology available to him, reasoned that it was God's judgment on the sins of his people.

The early church tried to fit it into an apocalyptic vision about the end of the world. [2]

These were our human attempts to make sense of the senseless, to give moral meaning to the tragic, to make intelligible a world become unintelligible. Think of the Jew trying to make sense of the world, of faith in God, after Auschwitz.

Now to Lisbon, 1755. It was the height of the Enlightenment, where nature was thought to be the perfect workings of the Creator and where European society was prospering by its ingenuity and enterprise.

Lisbon was the New York City of its day. A prosperous port city, called the Queen City of the Seas, it was the gateway to international exploration, trade, and colonization.

On November 1, 1755, the unimaginable happened. A huge earthquake struck the city. It lasted ten minutes. In an instant, thousands perished. The sky turned dark with dust. The earthquake was followed by terrible fires that raged across the city.

Then came a series of tidal waves that smashed into the port city: earth, fire, and water in relentless waves of destruction.

Vast wealth was lost, gold and silver in the millions; hundreds of valuable paintings by artists like Titian and Rubens were destroyed. Churches and palaces were in rubble. When it was over, fifteen thousand were dead. [3]

The Lisbon earthquake was said to shock Western civilization more than any event since the fall of Rome. Fifty years before, an earthquake had destroyed Port Royal, Jamaica, but there was no resulting "conceptual damage," no challenge to our basic ways of thinking. It was far away. Port Royal, Europeans said, was a city of pagans and half-breeds. They compared it to Sodom in the Old Testament: they had it coming to them.

But Lisbon, that jewel of European society? How to make sense of *this?*

Conservative theologians gloated: this was God's judgment on deism and liberal thinking, on greed and licentiousness. They couldn't, of course, explain why churches and bordellos were equally destroyed.

There were also moral judgments from the "left." One wrote:

> Think, O Spain, O Portugal, of the millions of poor Indians
> that your forefathers butchered for the sake of gold. [4]

Some preachers proclaimed this was God's call to repent before God brought greater disasters. Other preachers, reading texts like ours for today, announced that these were signs that the end of the world was near. So we'd better be prepared.

The earthquake also shook the assumptions of the intellectual world of the Enlightenment: A perfect creation created by the "Author of nature" (Rousseau). [5]

What now could we think? Immanuel Kant, all the way over in East Prussia, wrote three essays on earthquakes in the Königsberg newspaper. Rousseau and Voltaire added their voices. The great thinkers of Europe were challenged to rethink everything, as Auschwitz made us rethink everything in the twentieth century.

What resulted was that *the application of the moral category of evil could no longer be attached to nature.* The intelligible link between God, nature, and morality was broken. *Evil was now confined to the human and historical realms.*

Some suggest, thereby, that the modern era began at Lisbon.

Now to New York City. On September 11, 2001, the unthinkable happened to *us.* Two hijacked passenger planes flew into the Trade Towers. We watched what our minds at first could not comprehend. Then we watched the giant towers collapse floor by floor until there was nothing left of them, or of the nearly three thousand people trapped inside.

Conservative preachers took advantage of the catastrophe to make theological points and to advance their moral crusades: this was God's call to repent. Some announced that these were signs of the end of the world. You'd better get ready. Spiritual ambulance chasers.

Jerry Falwell and Pat Robertson responded with a moral viciousness not unusual for them, but which reached a new level of insensitivity in the wrenching aftermath of 9/11. On September 13, forty-eight hours after the disaster, Falwell and Robertson appeared on Robertson's *700 Club.* A transcript reads thus:

> Jerry Falwell: The ACLU's got to take a lot of the blame for this.... And, I know I'll hear from them on this. But throwing God out successfully with the help of the federal court system, throwing God out of the public square, out of the schools. The abortionists have got to bear some burden for this because God will not be mocked. And when we destroy forty million little innocent babies, we make God mad. I really believe the pagans, and the abortionists and the feminists, and the gays and lesbians who are actively trying to make that an alternative lifestyle, the ACLU, People for the American Way, all of them who have tried to secularize America, I point the finger in their face and say, "You helped this happen."

Pat Robertson replied: "Well, I totally concur."[6]

How can such words in the name of God possibly help? (Such words make me want to be a pagan, wear a pink triangle, preach in a dress, and join the ACLU.)

Of course, spokespersons from the Left had their own moral judgments to make and people to blame: the disaster was a result of American political and economic policies in the Middle East and around the world.

But these reactions come from old ways of thinking, and 9/11 is calling us, forcing us, to new ways of thinking.

Simplistic moral judgments from the Left or the Right will not do. Painting our enemies as evil and ourselves as righteous will not do. Old geopolitical formulas will not do.

There must a new consciousness arise: about the interconnectedness of everything; about the values *and* dangers of religion; about a way of making discerning ethical judgments and moral choices that have both conviction and modesty.

Can our texts from Isaiah and Luke help us?

Isaiah 62 urges us not to lose hope. Lift your heads and look for God's redemption that is coming! Your Babylonian captivity will one day end and you will go home. Your beloved Jerusalem will not be called A City Forsaken, but A City Sought Out.

Luke's text is more complex. Looking down at a page of the Gospels is like looking at a set of transparencies all laid one on the top of the other. You see multiple layers of history and tradition all at once.

You see historical happenings, remembered words of Jesus. You see Jesus' words paraphrased and applied. You see how the church—forty to fifty years after Jesus—heard the Risen Christ speaking a new word to them through the Spirit. It's all there.

In Luke 21 you see fragments of Jesus' sayings collected; you see a report of what happened to Jerusalem in 70 C.E.; you see a community trying to come to terms with that catastrophe; you see them appropriating the "Son of Man" sayings of Daniel and Jesus as they tried to make sense of it all.

That is why the text seems so impenetrable, so mystifying. Add to that the theological interpretations laid on top of these texts through the years—like the sub-Christian theology of the "Rapture"—and it's no wonder we scratch our heads and decide it might be better just to set the Bible aside.

Let me offer three words I hear the Spirit saying in these texts today:

First, I hear the people of God trying to make sense of catastrophe, trying to hang on to the hope that God will not abandon us, that God will find some way, with us or without us, to save us and to redeem all the world. This is our hope in God, in Christ.

Second, I hear the word of serious human responsibility for what happens. Just as we cannot blame God for earthquakes, neither can we blame God for human and historical evil. These catastrophes are not signs of the final pieces of an apocalyptic drama being played out, we the puppets, God the puppeteer.

Human evil is composed of human choices we make. And we are more apt to make evil choices when we think ourselves incapable of such. As seventeenth-century philosopher and mathematician Blaise Pascal noted in *Pensées*:

> Man is neither angel nor beast; and the misfortune is that he who would act the angel acts the beast.

Third, and last, "The Son of Man" language of Daniel and Jesus is given us to help us imagine and therefore believe in the full coming of the kingdom of God and the full redemption of the world.

It means God will not abandon us or abandon history. It means that God's mercy and truth and power will finally prevail and that the end of things will be the Great Amen, a Universal Homecoming for all God's children.

And it means an ethical challenge: that we live *now* in the presence of the Messiah, in the ways of the Son of Man and by the values of the kingdom Jesus preached. Beneath all the mystifying language of Daniel and Revelation and Luke 21 is the message: Live God's future today!

Mark Twain once said, "It's not the parts of the Bible I *don't* understand that give me trouble; it's the parts of the Bible I *do* understand."

Of all of Jesus' sayings about the Son of Man, this one is the most clear: Matthew 25:31-46. When the Son of Man comes in glory and sits on the throne, Jesus said, he will not ask, What's your theology, your denomination, your political persuasion? The questions will be: did you take in the stranger; feed the hungry; give water to the thirsty; clothe the naked; visit the prisoner? This is Ground Zero Spirituality.

Last spring I went to a theological conference in New York City, a few blocks from Ground Zero, and walked around the site for the first time. It's impossible to express all I felt as I looked at that giant jagged hole in the middle of the city. Then I walked a block away to a famous old church, St. Paul's Chapel, built in 1766. George Washington worshiped there. There is still a pew prominently marked where he sat: Washington's pew.

It is the oldest public building in continuous use in New York City. It is perfect Georgian Colonial architecture, a priceless architectural treasure. It looks very much like our sanctuary. To walk into it is to feel at home.

As a historical landmark it had been perfectly preserved. Before 9/11 you couldn't put a thumbtack in the wall or a piece of tape without an act of Congress—or vote of the Session, which was harder.

Then came 9/11. Somehow the church survived intact, not even a window broken. They say a large century-old sycamore tree took the brunt of the blast and saved the church at the cost of its life. Imagine that.

The church, however, was reborn that day in the crucible of the devastation. It became headquarters, hospital, resting place, and sanctuary for the emergency workers who would work for months in the horrifying rubble next door trying to save lives, recover bodies, and clear the site. Fifteen hundred people were fed every day for all those months.

The eighteenth-century fence and gate outside the church became covered with posters and pictures, mementos, and articles of clothing memorializing the lost. Inside, the sanctuary became the emergency shelter and temporary home for firefighters and police and other emergency workers. The hallowed pew of George Washington became the "foot clinic," where podiatrists treated the tired and damaged feet of workers. Pews became massage tables, counseling rooms. Firefighters slept and rested in full gear on pews, their shoes and belts gouging into the wood, scarring the pews.

Every square inch of available wall space in the sanctuary was covered with posters and cards from all over the world. A makeshift altar was built with an icon of Saint Paul sent by a Russian Orthodox church. One poster, which was attached to a column, read in large letters "You Ran In When We All Ran Out."

When you go to St. Paul's Chapel today you see a gallery of photos, books, tapes, remembrances of those days. Outside on the eighteenth-century fence is still a fireman's boot, remembering one of the fallen.

And the pews inside are all cleaned up now for public worship. But the scars in the wood are still there.

The church decided when they cleaned the pews not to refinish or repaint them. They wanted the scars to remain as a witness to those days of calamity and to a church reborn in the ashes of 9/11.

When I was there that day, I felt the scars in the wood with my hand. I still do. This is Ground Zero Spirituality.

When the Son of Man comes, Jesus said, he will not ask the church, What is your theology? or, How many members? He'll say, "Where are your scars?"

CHAPTER FOURTEEN

THE REVELATORY CRISIS OF ABU GHRAIB PRISON

It's still too soon to declare the Iraq mission a failure . . . it's not too early to begin thinking about what was clearly an intellectual failure. There was, above all, a failure to understand the consequences of our power. . . . Far from being blinded by greed, we were blinded by idealism.
—David Brooks, New York Times, May 11, 2004

If virtue becomes vice through some hidden defect in the virtue; if strength becomes weakness because of the vanity to which strength may prompt the mighty man or nation; if security is transmuted into insecurity because too much reliance is placed upon it; if wisdom becomes folly because it does not know its own limits—in all such cases the situation is ironic.
—Reinhold Niebuhr, The Irony of American History

Nothing is covered up that will not be uncovered, and nothing secret that will not become known. Therefore whatever you have said in the dark will be heard in the light, and what you have whispered behind closed doors will be proclaimed from the housetops. —Luke 12:2-3

Alas for those who are at ease in Zion, and for those who feel secure on Mount Samaria. . . . Are you better than these kingdoms? Or is your territory greater than their territory, O you that put far away the evil day, and bring near a reign of violence? —Amos 6:1-3

*This sermon, preached June 27, 2004, explores the moral quandary raised by the issue of torture at Abu Ghraib prison.

There are moments the Bible calls revelatory moments, apocalyptic moments. Apocalypse means an "unveiling" or "revealing." Suddenly so. In these moments we see the truth about God and the truth about us.

I call the sermon "The Revelatory Crisis of Abu Ghraib Prison." In the New Testament the word for crisis and judgment is the same, *krisis*. It means a time when the truth is revealed and choices must be made.

Abu Ghraib is such a crisis. It can lead us to the truth; or it can chase us farther into darkness.

Of all the horrifying pictures of prisoners beaten, threatened by guard dogs, stripped and sexually humiliated, the most haunting image to me is the man stretched out against a wall like a scarecrow; it looks like a crucifixion. He is standing on a box; he is naked except the black cloth draping his body and a black hood over his head. Electrical wires are attached to his hands. He is like a man being crucified, only he is a Muslim, and "Christians" are doing the crucifying.

The image reminds me of Marc Chagall's 1938 painting, *White Crucifixion*. In the center is the crucified Jesus, naked except for a Jewish prayer cloth, a *tallith*, around his loins. Circling the figure are scenes from the holocaust where Nazis in their perverted form of Christianity destroy synagogues and persecute and kill Jews.

The image from Abu Ghraib could be called "Black Crucifixion." And not just because of the color of the cloth and hood.

Seymour Hersh, reporting on the Abu Ghraib abuses, links it to a longer and broader effort of American Military Intelligence to use whatever means necessary to get more information from detainees in the fight against terrorism. The Defense Department initiative was a secret one. The military intelligence officers operated in what they called a "black zone," meaning no one would ever know, and no one would have to be responsible or accountable. But black zones cannot last forever. As Jesus said:

For there is nothing hidden, except to be brought to light; nor anything secreted away that won't be exposed. (Mark 4:22)

I walk in risky territory here. A prophet in the biblical sense always places himself or herself among the accused, not as their divine accuser. As Isaiah cried out, "I am a man of unclean lips, and I dwell among a people of unclean lips" (Isa. 6:5).

Given certain circumstances, I am capable of doing anything and everything those involved have done, from the guards in the picture to those up the chain of command who opened the door to such abuse. I am more like them than unlike them. And I, as an American, inescapably share in the responsibility of what has been done.

There are moments in all of our lives when these words of Jesus come true. In Luke's version:

Nothing is covered up that will not be uncovered, and nothing secret that will not become known. Therefore whatever you have said in the dark will be heard in the light, and what you have whispered behind closed doors will be proclaimed from the housetops. (Luke 12:2-3)

Or in the simplest, and perhaps earliest, version from the Gospel of Thomas:

For there is nothing hidden that will not be revealed. (Thomas 5:2)

Jesus was speaking of those revelatory moments, those apocalyptic moments when what has been hidden will suddenly be exposed. In light of Jesus' teaching on the "kingdom of God"—which was the subject of *all* his preaching—these words suggest this to me:

When the kingdom of God draws near—and it is always drawing near—it comes near in *judgment and mercy*. It shows us God's dream for the world and it reveals how far we've fallen from that ideal. And in this revelatory moment, it gives us a new chance to join in what God is doing.

There are many moral lessons to be learned in light of the Abu Ghraib abuse. Here are some.

1. *The ends do not justify the means.* Even in war there are internationally recognized restraints on behavior. In this case, the Geneva Conventions.

The treacherous slope to moral chaos is the reasoning that goes something like this: if the goal is good enough, then any means can be justified to reach that goal.

We see such moral error in all arenas of American life: business, politics, religion, sports, education. We cheat on exams; we cheat with performance-enhancing drugs in sports; we cheat on financial reports; in politics lying has become an art form perfected by media technology.

Jesus taught that in the kingdom of God, the ends do not justify the means. The means must be consistent with the ends. In fact, in the kingdom the ends are present in the means themselves.

2. *What is done in secret will be revealed; in one way or another it will be revealed.* Sometimes our secrets are publicly exposed. Other times our secrets become our prison. They reveal themselves in the price our bodies and minds pay.

Some may rightly object that there are some secrets necessary in the realm of national defense. But these are secrets we have commonly agreed to be necessary, and there are checks and balances set up to monitor what is made secret. These checks and balances are now being tested.

3. *We need to live by moral principles that are not subject to circumstance and situation.* Jesus' Golden Rule is a good starting place: "Do unto others as you would have them do unto you." Or Rabbi Hillel's version: "Do not do to others what you would not have them do to you."

Immanuel Kant in the eighteenth century offered what he called his "categorical imperative": when faced with a moral choice, ask, "What if *everyone* did as I plan to do?"

4. *There is right and wrong, and we don't get to make the rules.* God said to Amos: I have placed a plumb line in your midst so that you can tell what is right and what is wrong, what is crooked and what is straight.

We cannot always discern this plumb line, and none of us is good enough to live up to it every day, but to live as if there were no plumb line throws us into moral chaos, a kind of spiritual vertigo.

One of the most alarming things about Abu Ghraib is that it appears that it has happened in a larger context in which American leaders have claimed the right to decide when we need to observe the Geneva Conventions and when we do not. We have declared a "War on Terrorism," and we have extended that war into a preemptive war in Iraq, but we say this is a new kind of war and the old rules do not apply. We define who are "lawful combatants" and who are "unlawful combatants." We define what is "torture" and what is not.

In the *National Security Strategy* document,[1] produced by the White House and the National Security Council September 2002, it is stated: "We will take the actions necessary to ensure that our efforts to meet our global security commitments and protect Americans are not impaired by the potential for investigations, inquiry, or prosecution by the International Criminal Court whose jurisdiction does not extend to Americans and which we do not accept."

Furthermore, it says: "While the United States will constantly strive to enlist the support of the international community, we will not hesitate to act alone, if necessary, to exercise our right to self-defense by acting preemptively against such terrorists."

I am sure there are carefully articulated reasons for such assertions, but my soul cries out: are there any rules or principles beyond our own counsel and desires by which we seek to act? Are we, as a nation, a "law unto ourselves"?

Kenneth Roth, executive director of Human Rights Watch, says that we are "giving the world a ready-made excuse to ignore the Geneva Conventions." Have we not already given any nation the ready-made excuse to engage in its own preemptive war?

5. President Reagan loved to quote John Winthrop, the first governor of the Massachusetts Bay Colony: "For we must consider that we shall be as a city on a hill, the eyes of all people are upon

us." *What Abu Ghraib shows the world is not our light, but rather our shadow side of racism, rankism, and religious imperialism.*

When Rev. James A. Forbes Jr. visited our church, he described our foreign policy as a "supremacist foreign policy." The phrase should startle us into self-examination. In light of Abu Ghraib, I ask, Would we have treated German or Russian, Caucasian, or Christian prisoners the way we treated these Arab and Muslim prisoners?

The episode also demonstrates a new word I learned this week: "rankism." It is defined this way: rankism is the abuse of power inherent in rank. One "pulls rank" when one uses rank to diminish or exploit another.

"It happens every day," writes former President of Oberlin College, Robert Fuller: "A boss harasses an employee. A customer demeans a waiter. A coach bullies a player. A doctor disparages a nurse. A teacher humiliates a student. A parent belittles a child." [2]

We all have the capacity for this. Mark Bowden, writing in the *Atlantic Monthly* about Abu Ghraib, says: "People don't like to admit it, but the propensity for cruelty is in all of us, and it rises to the surface for many when they are given complete authority over other human beings." [3]

What Abu Ghraib has reinforced in the minds of many Muslim people is their worst fears about America—that we are a morally decadent society, that we are a *jahilyyah*, a culture of moral decay, which can only be overcome by *jihad*, holy war.

Karl Rove, the chief political strategist of President Bush, has said that it will take a generation to repair Abu Ghraib's damage to America's image with the Middle East.

6. *"Obeying orders" is no moral or legal defense.* We took this position as a nation at the Nuremberg Trials. It applies to us as well.

7. *Sometimes, therefore, we must for the sake of conscience stand apart.* We have seen in business, politics and at Abu Ghraib heroic individuals who have seen morally abhorrent behavior by their peers and superiors and have chosen to blow the whistle, often at great personal cost. If someone above you is asking of you things which

are morally objectionable to you, get out of that situation, stand apart, and report it so that the behavior does not continue.

8. The last point is the most complex. I call upon the help of David Brooks, conservative political analyst, and Reinhold Niebuhr, perhaps the greatest American theologian of the twentieth century. The point, in one sentence: *Respect the limits of human power, wisdom, and virtue.*

David Brooks, who has been a strong advocate of the war in Iraq, wrote in the *New York Times* on May 11, 2004: "It's still too soon to declare the Iraq mission a failure . . . it's not too early to begin thinking about what was clearly an intellectual failure. There was, above all, a failure to understand the consequences of our power. . . . Far from being blinded by greed, we were blinded by idealism."[4] We thought if our power were sufficient and our motive good, that is, the overthrowing of a malevolent dictator, all would work out smoothly and well.

Reinhold Niebuhr pondered the same issues in the early 1950s in America when our power in the world had first become preeminent. "We take, and must continue to take, morally hazardous actions to preserve our civilization," he wrote. "We must exercise power." But we must do so with clear-eyed recognition of the *ironic* conditions of power: "If virtue becomes vice through some hidden defect in the virtue; if strength becomes weakness because of the vanity to which strength may prompt the mighty man or nation; if security is transmuted into insecurity because too much reliance is placed upon it; if wisdom becomes folly because it does not know its limits—in all such cases the situation is ironic."[5]

Our misjudgments about the use of our power and the success of our mission in Iraq came from a refusal to acknowledge the human limits of our power, wisdom, and virtue. The increased use of abusive military intelligence techniques appears to have come from our frustrations in not being able to reach our goals as easily or safely as we wanted.

Niebuhr wrote with a clear-eyed critique about the monstrous evil of Communism, but he also warned his own nation about the blindness of pride and power. There are moments when the frustrations of history tempt us to act imprudently. In 1952 he warned that such frustration might lead a nation to engage in "preventive war," though at that time he did not think a democratic society would tolerate preventive war. Both preemptive war and the abuse of prisoners at Abu Ghraib come from a nation's leaders who "lose patience with the torturous course of history."[6]

Irony happens when our idealism blows up in our face, when "human limitations catch up with human pretensions,"[7] when we fail "to recognize the limits of [our] capacities of power, wisdom and virtue."[8]

Niebuhr writes that even the most "Christian" civilization or most pious church needs to be reminded that: "The true God can be known only where there is some awareness of a contradiction between divine and human purposes, *even on the highest level of human aspirations.*"[9] This is what the prophet Jeremiah was getting at when he prophesied:

> Thus says the LORD: Do not let the wise boast in their wisdom, do not let the mighty boast in their might, do not let the wealthy boast in their wealth; but let those who boast boast in this, that they understand and know me, that I am the LORD; I act with steadfast love, justice, and righteousness in the earth, for in these things I delight, says the LORD. (Jer. 9:23-24)

Against the pretensions of nations is Psalm 2: "The One in heaven laughs; the LORD scoffs at them." In the eyes of God, the prophet Isaiah says, the nations are "like a drop from a bucket, and are accounted as dust on the scales" (Isa. 40:15).

So in light of our present situation, where America must exercise power but must exercise it as a nation that recognizes the limits of our power and wisdom and moral idealism, we hear the words of Amos:

> Alas for those who are at ease in Zion, and for those who feel secure on Mount Samaria . . . Are you better than these [other] kingdoms? Or is your territory greater than their territory, O you that put far away the evil day, and bring near a reign of violence? (Amos 6:1-3)

CHAPTER FIFTEEN

A DEEPER PATRIOTISM

When they had brought them, they had them stand before the council. The high priest questioned them, saying, "We gave you strict orders not to teach in this name, yet here you have filled Jerusalem with your teaching and you are determined to bring this man's blood on us." But Peter and the apostles answered, "We must obey God rather than any human authority." —Acts 5:27-29

When in the Course of human events, it becomes necessary for one people to dissolve the political bands which have connected them with another, and to assume among the powers of the earth, the separate and equal station to which the Laws of Nature and of Nature's God entitle them, a decent respect to the opinions of mankind requires that they should declare the causes which impel them to the separation. . . . And for the support of this Declaration, with a firm reliance on the protection of divine Providence, we mutually pledge to each other our Lives, our Fortunes and our sacred Honor. —A reading from *The Declaration of Independence*

*This sermon, preached July 4, 2004, addresses allegiance to God and to country on our nation's Independence Day.

On this July 4, we celebrate the signing of the Declaration of Independence. It states the principles upon which our nation was founded and toward which our nation has set its course:

> We hold these truths to be self-evident, that all men are created equal, that they are endowed by their Creator with certain unalienable Rights, that among these are Life, Liberty and the pursuit of Happiness.

Of course we were not ready to live into the full implications of these words. Thomas Jefferson, who wrote its words, owned during his lifetime from 150 to 200 African American slaves. Women would not get to vote for over a century, and today we are still trying to hammer out civil rights equality for gay and lesbian people.

All people and every period of history have their blind spots. What God intends for us and for the world lies not behind us in some golden age, but ahead of us in a future being shaped even now by the Spirit of God.

God was seen to be in the founding of our nation and was prominently featured in our founding documents. It is consistent with our founding to have in our Pledge of Allegiance the words "one nation under God."

But the "God" involved in these early documents was a God shaped by the spirit of the times; and the spirit of the times, especially among the educated classes, fancied the theology of "deism."

If Calvinism had its five points—arranged in the acronym TULIP: Total Human Depravity, Unconditional Election, Limited Atonement, Irresistible Grace, and Perseverance of the Saints—so deism had its five points, outlined by Edward Herbert, Lord of Cherbury:
1) There is a God;
2) He ought to be worshiped;

3) Virtue is the principal element in the worship;
4) Humans should repent for their sin;
5) There is a life after death, where evil will be punished, and the good rewarded. [1]

Thomas Paine was the most famous—and infamous—propagator of deism in America. Teddy Roosevelt later called him a "filthy little atheist." But as a credo in his most famous book, *The Age of Reason*, he wrote:

> I believe in one God, and no more; and I hope for happiness beyond this life. I believe in the equality of man and I believe that religious duties consist in doing justice, loving mercy and endeavoring to make our fellow-creatures happy. [2]

Deism was not atheistic. But its God was remote: the Creator, the Architect, the overarching Providence. It distrusted religion, disbelieved in the supernatural, and was subtly anti-Semitic.

Benjamin Franklin, raised in New England Puritanism, found a happy home in deism. He wrote:

> Here is my Creed. I believe in one God, Creator of the Universe: That he governs the World by his Providence. That he ought to be worshiped. That the most acceptable Service we can render to him is doing good to his other Children. That the Soul of Man is immortal, and will be treated with Justice in another life, respecting its Conduct in this. These I take to be the fundamental Principles of all sound Religion. [3]

George Washington was a deistic Episcopalian who was a regular worshiper but was never confirmed and avoided Holy Communion. [4] Evangelical writers as early as 1800 tried to paint a picture of Washington as extremely pious, using anecdotes as reliable as the cherry tree story.

John Adams was a Christian deist, a Congregationalist by denomination. His wife, Abigail, was the daughter of a

Congregationalist minister. He called himself "a church-going animal" and attended church twice on Sundays.

He wrote to Jefferson that the abuses of religion had tempted him twenty times in his reading of late to say that the world would be better off without religion but that in the end he had concluded:

> Without Religion this World would be something not fit to be mentioned in polite company, I mean Hell. [5]

On to Thomas Jefferson. While he was a true son of the Enlightenment, religion was of great interest to him. One historian wrote that religion "mesmerized him, enraged him, tantalized him, alarmed him, and sometimes inspired him."[6] Baptized into the Church of England, he avidly read deist thought. He attended church regularly and even invented a fold-up stool to use when he went to church services. He valued greatly the ethics of Jesus and compiled his own gospel of Jesus, which emphasized Jesus' moral teachings and excluded miracles. He could have started his own Jesus Seminar.

This is a terribly short summary, and I hope not misleading. We should always assume when studying an earlier historical period that there is far more we *cannot* understand than we *can*. As L. P. Hartley wrote in his novel *The Go-Between*: "The past is a foreign country. They do things differently there."[7]

This summary serves to remind us that there were important spiritual/theological underpinnings to the founding principles of our nation. These were broad principles not to be confused with specific church doctrine. What Jefferson called "religious opinions" had no place in public life.

The First Amendment to the U.S. Constitution made sure that the state would not "establish" any particular religion and that religion would be "free" from government intrusion.

If there was a "wall of separation" between church and state, it was meant to be a *porous* wall, like those modern fabrics that are designed to let some things through but not other things. The free exchange of moral and ethical principles should pass back and forth, between religion and government, but religious doctrine and sectarian interpretation of scripture should not pass from the realm of religion to the realm of the state. And the state should not favor any church's interpretation of scripture in order to win political power.

The wall of separation is an intentionally porous wall: it lets some things pass through but not others. It is a woven wall: it is woven by human hands and needs at times to be rewoven. But it is still a wall, one that distinguishes the unique experiment in representative democracy that is the United States. It avoids both theocracy and a values-free secularism.

The moral and ethical issues which should be part of public discourse and the making of laws should be "self-evident" to the citizens, and not the special knowledge religions claim to have been "revealed" to them by God. Moral virtues should be hammered out in the public square, no religion or philosophy having a trump card, and may the best morals win!

For such reasons I am in favor of phrases like "one nation under God," in our Pledge of Allegiance.

But with an important proviso: that the "God" we are "under" is acknowledged as the God of all persons, all life, all religions and that we vigorously maintain freedom of religion and the freedom of citizens not to be religious. Otherwise the phrase "*one nation under God*" is an oxymoron.

I also like the phrase *because it promotes, or should, the personal virtue of humility and the political virtue of reverence.* That is, it serves to remind us that *we* are not God and that none of us has the corner on truth or morality.

Far from being a trump card religious people can play to assert their moral superiority, the phrase "under God" should serve to make us a nation that bows beneath the mystery of God and recognizes the human limits to our wisdom and virtue. (Abraham Lincoln is, as seen above, an exemplar.)

Our nation is *still being formed*, still being led on by God to fulfill our brightest dreams and to embody our best ideals.

Our dreams and ideals are best realized when we practice what we preach in the Declaration of Independence: the authority of government rests in "the consent of the governed." The genius of democracy is that it takes into account both the human capacity for good and the human capacity for evil. Reinhold Niebuhr said our capacity for justice makes democracy possible and an inclination to evil makes democracy necessary. So Thomas Jefferson urged general education as a tool for citizens to keep vigilant watch over their government.

Baptists have historically stood for religious freedom and political dissent, though many "Baptists" today hanker after a cozier relationship between church and state. We have upheld the sanctity of conscience and supported the freedom of those who by conscience have opposed certain laws and policies of their nation. Religious freedom and political freedom grow inextricably together in the same soil. Pull up one by its roots and you pull up the other.

In Acts 5:27-29, we see the early courage of the apostles to defy government and religious authorities and to practice nonviolent resistance. "We must obey God rather than any human authority," they said, "God, not man."

Sometimes God and country compel us to the same acts of duty and allegiance to the nation. We should never forget nor fail to give thanks for those who have given their lives for the sake of our freedom and for the freedom of other peoples.

Other times God and country create in us a crisis of conscience, and we must choose to follow God and resist the policies and laws of our nation. That was how our nation began as we broke our political bands with England.

The Civil Rights movement was a nonviolent revolution in America that succeeded in overturning laws and practices that discriminated against African Americans. It was led by the African American church and by its Moses and our Moses, Martin Luther King Jr.

This sermon is a call to a "deeper patriotism." Such a patriotism works to help America live up to its most cherished ideals.

124

We love our nation, right and wrong, but we love it too much to let it wander too long or too far from the right path. In *The Defendant*, G. K. Chesterton's classic work, he wrote: "To say, 'My country right or wrong'... is like saying, 'My mother drunk or sober.'"

Such deeper patriotism announces our first allegiance to God, believing that in serving God we will be serving the truest ideals of our nation, for our nation was founded on truths of God imbedded in the fabric of creation and the human soul.

A gaggle of political and religious leaders once came to Jesus. They tried to trap him by asking him to comment on a highly explosive political and religious issue: Should Jews pay taxes to the Roman emperor? Jesus turned the question back to them and to us:

> Give therefore to the emperor the things that are the emperor's, and to God the things that are God's. (Matt. 22:21)

Chew on that one, he said. We still do.

We who love our nation and love God are called to deeper patriotism. It keeps us a restless, reverent, hopeful, humble, idealistic, questioning, valiant, and loyal people who sing:

America! America!
God mend thine every flaw,
Confirm thy soul in self-control,
Thy liberty in law.

CHAPTER SIXTEEN

HOW TO BE CHRISTIAN IN AN ELECTION YEAR

> *Believing with you that religion is a matter which lies solely between man and his god, that he owes account to none other for his faith or his worship, that the legitimate powers of government reach actions only, and not opinions, I contemplate with sovereign reverence that act of the whole American people which declared that their legislature should make no law respecting an establishment of religion, or prohibiting the free exercise thereof, thus building a wall of separation between church and state.*
> —From a letter from President Thomas Jefferson

> *Congress shall make no law respecting an establishment of religion, or prohibiting the free exercise thereof; or abridging the freedom of speech, or of the press; or the right of the people peaceably to assemble, and to petition the Government for a redress of grievances.*
> —Amendment 1 to the Constitution, ratified December 15, 1791

> *I argue that the church gives no gift to the world in which it finds itself more politically important than the formation of a people constituted by the virtues necessary to endure the struggle to hear and speak truthfully to one another.*
> —Stanley Hauerwas

> *Only, live your life [politeuesthe] in a manner worthy of the gospel of Christ . . .* —Philippians 1:27

*This sermon, preached on July 11, 2004, addressed the growing political acrimony in a hotly contested election year.

127

I remember with vividness hot summer nights as a boy sitting on my grandfather's front porch listening with the adults to the Republican and Democratic conventions on radio. I heard the speeches and the roll call votes when Eisenhower and Adlai Stevenson won their party's nomination, when Nixon defeated Rockefeller for the Republican nomination, and when Kennedy won the Democratic nomination.

My grandfather, a grocer, was a Democrat. My other grandfather, a Baptist preacher, was, I suspect, a Republican, but he never spoke of it, playing his politics close to his vest.

Jesus was careful not to become a political Messiah—though the lure was always there. He preached a spiritual gospel that had political implications, not a political gospel with spiritual implications. At least that's how I read him.

It is not impossible to be Christian in an election year—but it's harder. We go through the every four-year cycle of messianism in which we are tempted to believe that God will come riding in on a ballot box. In such a season it's so easy to get caught up in that "work of the flesh" Paul called party spirit (Gal. 5:20)—which does not refer to being a "party-animal" but rather to the human inclination to divide up into fractious groups and to give yourself over to partisan rancor. Partisan passions rise to an even higher temperature in an election year.

So I preach on "How to Be Christian in an Election Year."

There is an interesting sentence in Paul's letter to the Philippians. Philippi was a prominent colony of Rome, and civic language was part of the *lingua franca*. Paul writes: "Let your manner of life (in the Greek, *politeuesthe*), your politics, your citizenship be worthy of the gospel of Christ" (Phil. 1:20).

He went on to suggest that Christians have dual citizenship, citizenship in our nation and citizenship in the kingdom of God: "But our citizenship, (our *politeuma*, our commonwealth) is in heaven, and it is from there that we are expecting a Savior, the Lord Jesus Christ" (Phil. 3:20). It is worth noting that in Philippi and in the Roman Empire at that time the Roman emperor expected people to say "*Caesar* is Lord."

So first, we acknowledge our dual citizenship as Christians and reaffirm that our primary allegiance is to Christ and citizenship in the kingdom of God. We are in trouble when being Republican or Democrat is more important than our baptism.

Baptist theologian Clyde Fant told in a sermon, "Uncle Sam and Jesus: In That Order" of his wife's trip to her hometown in Beaumont, Texas, where she went with her mother to her Baptist church on July 4 for a patriotic religious service. There were three flagpoles outside the church, the one in the middle towering over the other two. On the flagpoles were the Christian flag, the American flag, and the Texas flag. Fant reported: "Jesus and Texas tied for second."

Second, we honor the American principle of the separation of church and state. The principle is carved into our civic life in the First Amendment of the United States Constitution. There it is: freedom of religion included along with freedom of speech, freedom of the press, freedom of assembly and petition.

We are always tempted to discard this principle. The church craves the support of the state for its religious and moral purposes, and the state craves the support of the church to achieve its political ends.

Having said that, I should also say that the doctrine of the separation of church and state is a *nuanced* doctrine. It forbids the establishment of a theocracy on the one hand; on the other hand it does not drive religion out of the public square and create a secular state devoid of religious influence. It is not the theocracy of Iran's Ayatollah Khomeini. Nor is it France's aggressively secular state.

There is a "wall of separation" between religious institutions and the state. Baptists fought for this principle with their lifeblood, not only for themselves but also for all people of all religions and of no religion.

Our American founders fought for this principle. James Madison is quoted as saying that "the separation of church and state is to keep forever from these shores the ceaseless strife that has soaked the soil of Europe with blood for centuries."

Thomas Jefferson was the first to use the expression "wall of separation." He did so in a carefully written letter responding to the Danbury Baptist Association, which asked why he did not establish national days of fasting and thanksgiving as Washington and Adams had done before him. We have the several drafts of the letter he mailed on January 1, 1802. He knew how important the issue was. At the time, he was being accused of being an atheist by the opposing political party, the Federalists, because of his unorthodox theology and his defense of the separation of church and state. In the letter he quoted the First Amendment to the Constitution and used the metaphor of "a wall of separation between church and state."

The phrase has become a political and judicial football of late. Supreme Court Justice William Rehnquist has called it a "misleading metaphor." David Barton, founder and president of WallBuilders and vice-chair of the Texas Republican Party, has written a book, *The Myth of Separation,* in which he asserts that "the separation of church and state" is a misreading of the founders' true intentions for America. He wants America "reconstructed" as a "Christian nation." There have been two bills introduced by Congress the last two years to permit greater partisan political activity by churches and ministers, bills named euphemistically "The Houses of Worship Speech Protection Act" and "The Church Safe Harbor for Churches Act." They should have been called "Wolves in Sheep's Clothing Acts." Our own North Carolina Congressman Walter Jones has led the charge in support of them. Thankfully these have been defeated.

The "wall of separation" has been one of the great monuments in human society's history. It is part of the genius of American democracy, and it is one of the reasons for religious vitality in America. It has kept religion free from the taint of governmental power and kept government free from the blindness that religious zealotry can bring.

But as I have suggested earlier, the "wall of separation" is a *porous* wall, like those new fabrics carefully designed to let some elements pass back and forth but not others.

What should, what must, pass through are ethical and moral values. There should be rigorous and free conversation between religion and government about the moral and ethical values we want to help shape our personal lives and our social policy. Religious people should carry into the public square their moral values and ethical vision. But religious *institutions* should not get involved in political processes. The church needs to keep its sticky fingers off the state and the state needs to keep its sticky fingers off the church. When the two get together, something bad almost always happens.

Let me try to translate these principles to us here at Myers Park Baptist Church. As your minister, given by you a "free pulpit," I must be free to articulate moral and ethical principles as I see them relating to public and political issues. And by the same token, I must honor the "free pew" in which you sit, your right to disagree. For this reason I will not ask you as a *church* to take a position on a political or legislative matter. I may urge you as *individuals* to do so, but to do so frequently or carelessly would undermine my role as your minister.

We encourage our members to express their values in the political realm without dictating what they should do. We help our members announce opportunities for such expression—like the recent trip to talk to the state legislature about the moratorium on the death penalty.

Outside the church each of *you* has a "free pulpit" as priests of God in the world. Exercise that free pulpit. Let your conscience speak. God calls us to go into the public square and give voice to our most cherished moral convictions.

Take for a moment the moral principle of the "sacredness of life." For some this principle leads them to oppose the death penalty; for others this leads them to oppose Roe vs. Wade. It leads some to oppose child poverty and others to fight child pornography. It leads some to oppose the war in Iraq; it leads others to back the war.

A responsible church does not dictate moral response. It helps its congregants think through their moral commitments and flex their moral muscles. As God leads you, give voice to

your conscience. As we get involved in the public square, however, there are ways of doing so that can be more Christian and
less Christian.

So, a third point: Christians should recognize that the greatest
political act they can be part of is to *be the church*! That is, to
embody the kingdom of God in the midst of the kingdoms of this
world, the new creation in the midst of the old creation. This
may be the most radical part of the sermon and the least interesting part to you. To get busy in politics and fail to be the church
would be a grave unfaithfulness to Christ. Stanley Hauerwas
describes this being the church as "the formation of a people constituted by the virtues necessary to endure the struggle to hear
and speak truthfully to one another." [1] We can be such a place if
"I want to be right" is less important than *"I want to be truthful."*

A fourth point: As we enter the public square we do so with
the Christian virtue of humility. We claim the truth we've been
given but we don't claim to have all the truth. Our convictions
are tempered by an intellectual and spiritual humility. But humility
should not lead to timidity. It just keeps conviction from issuing
into arrogance.

You will hear a lot this fall about "values" and "faith" as they
relate to the candidates. Most of the talk will be by people who
have their own idea about what "faith" means or what "values"
means.

I have spoken in the past about how some churches have now
established "political tests" for membership and inclusion at the
Lord's Table. Bishops have forbidden Communion to Catholics
who support John Kerry. A Baptist pastor in North Carolina
invited those against President Bush to leave the church.

There also seem to have arisen "religious tests" for political
office, though the Constitution forbids such. A certain style of
faith seems to have become a litmus test for one's electability: a
kind of breezy, sunny, chatty evangelical faith. I believe one's
faith is a very important dimension of one's character, but I wish
just one candidate for major office would say when asked about
his or her faith: "My faith is a deep and formative part of who I
am. It shapes my character and informs my decisions. But it is far

too important a part of my life to be made the subject of sound bites and partisan politics. So, I will not talk about it. I hope you will see my faith in action and that you will judge my faith on the basis of my actions, not my actions on the basis of my faith."

Which leads to my fifth point. When Jesus commanded us to love our enemies, this includes—I hate to suggest it—the love of our political opponent. Where this begins is by *loving our enemy with our minds*. That is, we take care to try to understand why our opponents think the way they do.

So how can Democrats love Republicans with their minds and vice versa? One way is to understand how most of our moral and political virtues are *balancing* virtues. They complement each other and keep each other honest. Someone has defined a "heretic" as someone who has a complete grasp of a half-truth. We help keep each other from political heresies.

In our day, Republicans favor a small role for government and Democrats a large role. We need each other, or else government will try to do too *much* or too *little*.

In our day, Republicans tend to emphasize personal morality and individual virtue, while Democrats tend to emphasize social morality and civic virtue. We need each other, or else our moral vision will be too small.

In our day, Republicans emphasize the political virtue of "freedom" and the Democrats emphasize the political virtue of "equality." Freedom and equality are complementary virtues, not absolute virtues.

Republicans emphasize the personal freedom to achieve all one can achieve. Democrats emphasize equal opportunity and a level playing field.

"Freedom" left all to itself can end up in the law of the jungle and the survival of the fittest, fattest, and most privileged.

"Equality" left all to itself can end up in the totalitarian equality of communism, or in a culture which has lost all incentive for achievement.

We need each other and each other's competing and complementary virtues. This should not encourage moral and political complacency. It is a call to give voice to what is dearest to you. I think God will use that for the good.

Conclusion

I close with a hope for this church: that we can be a peculiar beacon of light in our world. That is, in a time when we are getting more and more polarized in America, we can be a safe harbor for diverse political and moral opinions. We can embody the "civility" politicians talk about but rarely practice.

David Brooks wrote recently in the *New York Times* about the growing cultural divide in America and about how people are enclosing themselves more and more in homogeneous groups where everyone thinks the same and votes the same.

We are a congregation with a generous amount of political and theological diversity, more than most congregations I know. Can this be a hallmark of our witness: that here is a place where liberals and conservatives and Democrats and Republicans can worship together and talk face to face about what is important to them?

If so, it means we must take special care to honor and understand those who take different positions. I lean a bit to the Left on most things, so I must take special care to listen to those of our congregation on the Right. The great South American archbishop Dom Helder Camara of Recife, Brazil, is attributed with saying, with a broad smile and thick accent: "Right hand, left hand—both belong to ze same body but ze heart is a little to ze left!" [2]

Some days my sermon raises the blood pressure of those on the Right, other days on the Left, some Sundays *both*. Perhaps those are the days I am best doing my job.

What I'm speaking of here is "our manner of life," the way in which we work and live together in community and in society, not just our "positions" and "opinions" but how we live with others' positions and opinions.

Paul's words to the Romans are a kind of church covenant for how to live together as the Body of Christ and how to live in society with those who are different. Listen to them again:

> Let love be genuine; hate what is evil, hold fast to what is good [Note: Paul says hate *what* is evil, not hate *who* is evil.]; love one another with mutual affection; outdo one another in showing honor. Do not lag in zeal, be ardent in spirit, serve the Lord.... Bless those who persecute you; bless and do not curse them.... Live in harmony with one another; do not be haughty, but associate with the lowly; do not claim to be wiser than you are. Do not repay anyone evil for evil, but take thought for what is noble in the sight of all. If it is possible, so far as it depends on you, live peaceably with all. Beloved, never avenge yourselves... Do not be overcome by evil, but overcome evil with good. (Rom. 12:9-21)

Let your manner of life, your politics, your citizenship be worthy of the gospel of Christ.

CHAPTER SEVENTEEN

THE CHURCH AT PRAYER AT ELECTION TIME

A s the 2004 Presidential election drew near and the divisions, political and cultural, were growing deeper, I called our church and our community to prayer with an Election Eve service of worship I called "A Community Service of Prayer for the Nation." As I introduced the service to the congregation, I said that it was a way we could express what Martin Marty called "the public church."[1]

I said this service would be one exercising one of the key callings of the church: prayer. Many of our people had been active in political campaigns, Republican and Democrat, during the past months. Now we would pray together—conservative and liberal, Democrat and Republican—sitting side by side at church. There would be no sermon, no speeches. The service would be composed of hymns, readings, scripture, and, mostly, prayer.[2]

The prayers for the community, state, and nation included the words: "We pray for our citizens going to the polls tomorrow, and we pray for all those whose names are on ballots. Grant us your wisdom, O God, and grant us grace in both winning and losing. Then create a new unity among us to work for the common good."

The closing hymn "This Is My Song," with words by Lloyd Stone and Georgia Harkness, was a perfect conclusion to the service. Set to the tune "Finlandia," it voices the prayer of a people who love their nation but also know God's love for all nations.

One of our members, Ed Williams, the editor of the editorial page of the *Charlotte Observer*, was there, no doubt wearied by the labors of his responsibility during the local, state, and national election season. He wrote about the service in an editorial dated November 3, 2004. The title of the editorial was "Prayers for Our Nation." Here is some of what he wrote:

My church held an election eve service to offer prayers for our community and nation. At the end of a nasty campaign, it was a cleansing experience.

My church, Myers Park Baptist, is not a patriotic institution. It is a Christian institution. We follow the will of God as we see it, regardless of whether that means supporting or opposing our national government's policy. The American flag does not fly in our sanctuary.

I am not saying our congregation isn't patriotic. The opposite is true. Our congregation includes current and former political officials, decorated veterans of many wars, activists of many political viewpoints, community volunteers, all of whom love America and cherish the values it stands for.

That was the tenor of Monday night's service. . . .

America has never been a perfect nation, but it always has been drawn by its founding ideals in the direction of justice. America's national commitment is that, as Lincoln said, we will proceed "with firmness in the right, as God gives us to see the right."

That is how God has blessed America. [3]

The week after the election, some of my congregation were downcast, others were elated. How do we handle all these feelings at church? On November 14, I chose to repeat the service of prayers as part of our morning worship. The sermon was titled "God and the Nations: How Does the Kingdom Come?" The texts were Isaiah 6:1-8 and Luke 17:20-21. Here is the sermon.

Our nation was founded upon a dream, or a set of dreams: Of a new experiment in human living and nationhood, of a new exercise in freedom and democracy that would be a light to the nations.

In 1630 en route to America aboard the *Arabella*, Governor John Winthrop wrote the famous words (see chapter 2):

> For we must consider that we shall be as a city on a hill, the eyes of all people are upon us.

We have watched our nation these two hundred plus years seek to become worthy of our dreams. The Civil War was a great testing ground to see whether we believed what we signed in the Declaration of Independence:

> We hold these truths to be self-evident, that all men are created equal.

In a speech to the New Jersey Senate in 1861, Abraham Lincoln spoke of our nation in the midst of this struggle as God's "almost chosen people." The words were a caution to politicians and preachers alike who assumed too quickly our chosenness by God and what that chosenness meant.

Presiding over a national calamity like the Civil War will either drive you deep or force you shallow. It drove Lincoln deep.

It has been a tumultuous three years for our nation since the day the towers fell. A savage attack by an enemy we scarcely knew or understood; a war on terrorism that would lead to a new doctrine of preemptive war and the war in Iraq; an uncertain economy; and a 50/50 nation whose political, cultural, and religious divisions have become sharper and more bitter.

If our land is to be healed of its deep divisions, faith communities must lead the way, but not in a way that smooths over the differences that now divide. Instead, we must lead in a way that listens deeply to our differences and calls us to a vision that transcends them, that brings out the best, not the worst in our differences, that calls upon the "better angels of our nature," to use Lincoln's words.

If a new unity is to happen in our nation, faith communities must lead the way. I say "faith communities" rather than "faith community" because we, too, are divided. Decades ago we spoke of the religious differences as between "Protestant, Catholic, and Jew." Today the divide seems to be between what we could call "traditional" Protestants, Catholics, and Jews on one side of the divide and "progressive" Protestants, Catholics, and Jews on the other. You may notice that I'm trying to avoid the F word, "fundamentalist," and the L word, "Liberal."

The deep structures of language, symbols, and behaviors are shifting like tectonic plates under the earth. We must seek a language that becomes a lamp, not a bludgeoning tool.

What are we to do as a faith community in such a time?

We are called to silence and to prayer. This may come as profound relief to a people inundated with words this past political season. Henri Nouwen says it well: "People expect too much from speaking, too little from silence."[4]

We are called to *prayer*, and this prayer may begin in wordlessness rather than in words.

In his poem "Little Gidding," T. S. Eliot wrote:

> You are not here to verify,/Instruct yourself, or inform curiosity/Or carry report. You are here to kneel.

The Archbishop of Canterbury Rowan Williams speaks of intercessory prayer as a kind of battle, a wrestling, an *agonia*, a struggle. It is, he says, "The struggle not to let God and the world fall apart from each other: because that is the centre of this prayer, the recognition that, in spite of appearances, God and the world belong together. There is no place where the love of God can't go."[5]

This kind of faith also sends us into the public sphere to *act*, to bring our best moral values into the public square, advocate for them, and let them be part of public debate.

The phrase "moral values" has become a hot topic since the exit polls on election day. Moral values are what *all* people bring to the public square, religious and secular, liberal and conservative:

- Freedom is a moral value—both political and religious freedom.
- The abolition of slavery was a moral value fought for by evangelicals, deists, and secularists alike.
- Full voting rights for women and blacks was a moral value.
- The protection of the life of the unborn is a moral value.
- The freedom of a woman to have final control of her body is a moral value.
- Concern about the family is a moral value.
- Equal civil rights for gay and lesbian families is a moral value.
- Just war—just cause of war and just conduct of war— is a moral value.
- The care for the most vulnerable in our nation is a moral value.
- The care for the environment is a moral value.
- Responsible fiscal policy that does not make debtors of our children is a moral value.

All God's people have moral values—and those *not* God's people, too, you will see if you read the Bible carefully.

But we must be careful *how* we bring our moral values to the public square. Moral values are by their nature passionately held values. But they do not mean "unexamined values." Both Left and Right need to examine their values. Our moral values do not trump others' values because we say they come from God. And moral values must be balanced with citizens' rights, no easy calculus.

We bring our moral values to the public debate. If and when they become sufficiently "self-evident" (to use Jefferson's phrase), then they shape public policy.

This past week, two texts have flooded into my heart and mind. The first is from Isaiah 6:

> In the year that King Uzziah died, I saw the Lord sitting on a throne, high and lofty. (Isa. 6:1)

If I had been a preacher the week President Kennedy was assassinated, that is the text I would have needed: some vision like that given to Isaiah, that in the midst of national calamity and uncertainty there is still a God who holds "the whole world in his hands."

As God's holiness is revealed, confession is wrenched from our hearts. With Isaiah we cry:

> Woe is me! I am lost, for I am a man of unclean lips, and I live among a people of unclean lips. (Isa. 6:5)

Could there be a truer confession for a nation after an election season when truth has been the casualty of political combat? We stand like Pilate before Jesus in chains and ask: "What is truth?" Where is the truth? Where can truth be found?

The currency of our language has been devalued because we've lost the gold standard of truth, because our speech has lost its connection to stubborn facts.

We may feel no need to confess if we compare ourselves to those across the political aisle, but now we are put next to the holiness of God. And we cry: Woe is me. I am a person of unclean lips and dwell amid a people of unclean lips.

A live coal is pressed to our lips. It is not an instrument of punishment, but an instrument of purification. Our singed lips for now cannot speak, but then we will speak truth, or at least the best and noblest truth we know.

Then God will say to us again, as persons and as a nation: "Whom shall I send, and who will go for us?" And we will say with Isaiah: "Here am I. Send me."

The other text is from Jesus' lips: two key phrases about the kingdom of God. The kingdom of God was the center of Jesus' preaching. The kingdom of God brings the values of God to earth: justice and righteousness, mercy, love, and peace. Every day we pray with Jesus, "Thy kingdom come, Thy will be done on earth as in heaven."

But we ask: *How* does the kingdom come? *Where* does the kingdom come? *When* does the kingdom come? We ask it fervently because our lives and the life of the world depend upon it. In Revelation, John, a member of a community being persecuted by the Roman emperor Domitian, cries out with his last words:

Amen. Come, Lord Jesus! (Rev. 22:20)

It is a prayer for the coming of the kingdom of God.

Jesus offers two important sayings about the kingdom for us today.

The first is this: *The kingdom comes not by observation* (Luke 17:20). It is a word of warning to us when we too easily identify our causes with the kingdom of God. Not so fast, Jesus says. The kingdom of God is not the Democratic Party or the Republican Party. Not red, not blue.

And it is a word of hope to those who despair about whether the kingdom will ever come. Jesus says: Don't give up. You can't always see where it makes its progress. It grows secretly; it advances even when you sleep.

The second word of Jesus is: *The kingdom of God is among you* (Luke 17:21). (*Entos* you, in the Greek, within you, in your midst.)

Here is a word of hope for those who yearn and wish, work and pray for the kingdom. The kingdom of God is not just future, it is *now*. It is not just out there; it is in *here*.

The kingdom is everywhere hearts are joined to God's heart, everywhere truth is found, everywhere justice rolls like waters, everywhere people pound out peace. It is where tyrants topple, and it is when you finally find your own God-given freedom. It is where the hungry are fed and marriages are mended and healing happens.

The kingdom is in your midst.

I closed the sermon with the same portions of Lincoln's Second Inaugural Address we read on election eve. I remember hearing of a prominent Southern Baptist preacher in the late nineteenth/early twentieth century who always seemed to figure out a way to get Robert E. Lee in his sermons. I think I could almost be accused of the same with Abraham Lincoln when preaching about the nation these days! But his words call us to a deeper, truer self and a deeper, truer patriotism in this time of national discord and international violence.

CHAPTER EIGHTEEN

COUNTY COMMISSIONERS, ROGER WILLIAMS, AND US

> *We suppose they went to Rhode Island, for that is the receptacle of all sorts of riff-raff people, and is nothing else but the sewer (latrina) of New England. All the cranks of New England retire thither.*
> —New Netherlands Minister on the refusal to allow Quakers in New Amsterdam

> *I desired it might be for a shelter for persons distressed for conscience.*
> —Roger Williams on why he founded Rhode Island as a colony of religious toleration

Recently I spoke at a county commissioners' meeting. I was there to speak as a minister in favor of a motion that protected gay and lesbian people from discrimination in county hiring practices. I suspected there would be plenty of Christians and Christian ministers lined up on the other side.

*This sermon, preached July 17, 2005, reflected on faith in the public square in the local Charlotte, North Carolina setting.

When I arrived, the room was packed: gay and lesbian people there in support of the motion; conservative and fundamentalist Christians there to oppose it.

The chairperson first allowed each commissioner to speak. One commissioner, who carries the fundamentalist torch in our city, read extensively from the Bible, interpolating his own interpretations as he went. He read almost every negative passage about homosexual acts he could find—and he found most of them. While he read I saw another commissioner rifling through a Bible. I thought to myself: "What is this? Civil magistrates arguing biblical interpretation and passing judgment on each other's Christian faith and moral rectitude?" It felt more like the church meeting from hell than a civil magistrates' meeting. Is this what we elect our public officials to do?

When the floor was opened for comments from the community, I went to the lectern to speak. I faced the commissioners and directly behind me was a sizable section of gay and lesbian people. I had watched as the county commissioner read the Bible at them, dishing out condemnation and wielding the Bible as a sword. I saw the shock and pain on their faces. I had felt the blows as in my own body. Now I, a Christian minister of the Baptist persuasion, was speaking on their behalf. Here is what I said:

Mr. Chairman, County Commissioners, I am Steve Shoemaker, senior minister of Myers Park Baptist Church. I thank you for this opportunity to speak and wish to voice my personal support for the motion to expand the category of protection against discrimination to include "sexual orientation."

We are struggling as a community and a nation with the age-old issue of how to be both virtuous and free. Virtue and freedom need each other. There is no true virtue that is not freely chosen; and freedom will not long endure without the virtues of its citizens.

When Roger Williams, the father of the Baptist movement in America, was banished from the Puritan Massachusetts Bay Colony in the 1630s, he founded Rhode Island as a colony of religious toleration. The issues involved had to do with what he called "soul liberty" and the limited sovereignty of government, that is, what we call "the separation of church and state." He also defended the land rights of

146

Native Americans, which did not endear himself to the colonists who believed that God had given them this new land.

Rhode Island became a haven for Baptists, Quakers, Congregationalists, Jews, Roman Catholics, and other persecuted minorities. Williams wrote that the "ship of state" should protect alike "Papists, and Protestants, Jews, and Turks." Thus it became an important feeder stream of American democracy.

What does Charlotte wish to be? A community driven by religious politics and politicized religion that tries to encode certain interpretations of scripture? Or will we be a thriving democracy, which values both virtue and freedom?

I have deep respect for religious leaders and congregations who interpret scripture differently than I on the issue of homosexuality. We differ in my own congregation. Can we liberal, conservative, Protestant, Catholic, Evangelical, Jew, and Muslim agree not to encode our biblical interpretations into civil law, thus turning the state into a church?

Homosexual persons indeed belong to those described in our Declaration of Independence: "We hold these truths to be self-evident, that all men are created equal, and that they are endowed by their Creator with certain unalienable Rights . . . Life, Liberty and the pursuit of Happiness."

There are those who would scoff at the expanding list of those protected from discrimination as a parody of an already disdained political correctness. It is, in fact, a roll call of honor, the ongoing human attempt of a community to act honorably and equitably toward all its citizens.

Thank you for this time to speak.

Happily, the motion passed six to three.

I had tried to temper my remarks, not wanting to add to the already tense and heated atmosphere. What I said to myself was, "Well, this is interesting. The magistrates are reading the Bible to me, and I'm reading the Declaration of Independence to them!" The night crystallized for me the difficult but important drama of American life today over the role of religion and politics.

First it underscored what I said at the beginning of my remarks that night: that what we are struggling with these days as a community and nation is the age-old question of how to be both virtuous *and* free, how to be a people embodying moral values and at the same time remain a secular democracy that respects religious pluralism and honors freedom of conscience. Or to put it this way, how to avoid theocracy on one end and on the other a radical secularism that dismisses religion or trivializes it.

I felt it important to identify myself as a Baptist minister. I was careful to say I spoke *personally*. What I said no doubt reflected on you, Myers Park Baptist Church, fairly and unfairly, but I wanted everyone to know I did not speak for you.

I felt it also important to invoke the name and historical witness of Roger Williams, not just because of his importance to the American tradition of the separation of church and state and religious liberty, but also because many Baptists today feel little qualm about their theocratic drift. They don't see what the big deal is about the separation of church and state and are all too ready to impose their moral values on everyone else.

So today a few more words about this man, the founder of the first Baptist church in America and the champion of religious freedom. If you go to Geneva, Switzerland, and see the memorial to the great Protestant reformers, he is the only American figure represented. Trained at Cambridge, ordained in the Church of England, he became part of the Puritan break from the Anglican Church and came to America to be a minister. It wasn't long before he began to make trouble. He objected to the right of magistrates to enforce "the first table of the law," the first half of the Ten Commandments that pertain to our relationship with God. (For example, non-Christians should not have to take an oath in court.) He protested the unlawful expropriation of land rightfully belonging to the Indians.

He saw the union of church and state as a manifestation of the situation in the book of Revelation; the Massachusetts Bay Colony he saw as "the ten kings which have received no kingdom as yet" but who wield beastly power over the faithful (Rev. 17:12). This did not make him the most popular preacher in the colony.

In his reading of scripture, the state had limited sovereignty. It had only to do with civil affairs. Jesus was the only one with kingly, absolute authority over the whole of our lives.

In October 1635, he was ordered to leave the Massachusetts Bay Colony. He set out in winter across the wilderness, bought land from the Narragansett Indians and began what would become the colony of Rhode Island. He wrote, *"I desired it might be for a shelter for persons distressed for conscience."* Later, Ann Hutchinson, a midwife and theologian, was likewise banished from Massachusetts and found in Williams's colony a place of refuge.

Not everyone had a positive view of what was going on in Rhode Island. A New Netherlands minister commented after Quakers were not allowed in New Amsterdam:

> We suppose they went to Rhode Island, for that is the receptacle of all sorts of riff-raff people, and is nothing else but the sewer (*latrina*) of New England. All the cranks of New England retire thither. [1]

In 1638, Williams joined with eleven others to found the first Baptist church in our nation. Within a year he left the Baptist church and called himself a "Seeker" because he believed the "true church" would only happen when Christ returned to earth. [2] He would continue to be of support to the Baptist congregation, but not be a member. Looking back, it seems a very "Baptist" kind of thing to do.

His friendship with Native Americans led him to defend their rights to their land. It also led to his publishing a book that explained the Indian language and Indian religion and culture: "A Key into the Language of America...Together with Brief Observations of the Customs, Manners and Worships..." Although a fervent follower of Jesus, he would not try to convert Indians to Christianity because he believed that under the circumstances such an effort would be a coercion of their conscience. [3]

The charter for Rhode Island, which he wrote and was granted from England in 1663, became a touchstone for the American tradition of religious freedom and separation of church and state.

Williams had an unstintingly prophetic message to his culture. "The truth is," he wrote,

> The great Gods of this world are God-belly, God-peace, God-wealth, God-honour, God-pleasure, etc. [4]

He was a follower of the way of Jesus of Nazareth, who, as he described in his seventeeth-century vernacular and spelling:

> disdained not to enter this world in a stable, amongs beasts, as unworthy the society of men: who past through this world with the esteeme of a mad man, a deceiver, a conjuror, a traytor against Caesar, and destitute of an house wherein to rest his head: who made choice of his first and greatest embassadours out of fisher-men, tent-makers, etc. and at last chose to depart on the stage of a pianfull shamefull gibbet. [5]

It was in the tradition of Roger Williams that I went to the county commissioners that night.

So in summation, I will close with a few questions to myself, a self-interview—which is my favorite kind.

Q: Steve, do you enjoy speaking at such places?

A: I think I enjoy it about as much as a colonoscopy without anesthesia.

Q: Then why did you go?

A: Because separation of church and state does not mean the separation of moral values and the government. In fact separation of church and state protects my right and freedom to bring my moral and spiritual values into the public square. Scripture urges us to seek the welfare of the city into which we've been placed (Jer. 29:7).

Q: How do you bring these values into the public square without violating the separation of church and state?

A: First, I speak to *issues*; I do not endorse parties or candidates. Secondly, while I voice support for certain values, I do not use the Bible and my interpretation of the Bible to make my case. I try to appeal to broader moral and spiritual values that can be shared by people of other faiths or of no faith. So in this case I read from the Declaration of Independence.

Q: *What were the moral values you presented that night?*

A: Jesus called us to take special care of "the little ones," those considered "least of these" in our society. And there is in Hebrew scripture a noble tradition of the nation protecting those most vulnerable in the society: the poor, orphans, widows, and "resident aliens," sometimes called foreigners or strangers—those we'd call immigrants today, people who live on the fringe of society.

Deuteronomy tells us that judges were chosen and charged with these words:

> Give the members of your community a fair hearing, and judge rightly between one person and another, whether citizen or resident alien. You must not be partial in judging: hear out the small and the great alike; you shall not be intimidated by anyone, for the judgment is God's. (Deut. 1:16-17)

And what is God's judgment like?

> For the LORD your God is God of gods and Lord of lords, the great God, mighty and awesome, who is not partial and takes no bribe, who executes justice for the orphan and the widow, and who loves the strangers, providing them food and clothing. You shall also love the stranger, for you were strangers in the land of Egypt. (Deut. 10:17-19)

Translated to our day, I was there to support gay and lesbian people who have been and are on the receiving end of bigotry and discrimination. There are laws today that discriminate against gay and lesbian persons that are relics of a time in the past in which the biblical interpretation by those in power was made into civil law. I was there to argue that when this happens, the state is trying to be the church.

There are civil laws that are based on the Ten Commandments, against murder and stealing, for example, but these have been made into law because the general populace agrees that these are general moral values shared by most in our nation.

Sometimes in the moral growth of the nation we become newly sensitized to certain moral issues and change our laws, for example, slavery and women's rights. Today we are reexamining issues like homosexuality and capital punishment. And we are acknowledging the intense moral quandary of abortion in terms of the competing moral goods of the sacredness of life and the sacredness of a mother's right to choose what happens to her body. (It seems we never make progress on the issue of war.)

People of religious and ethical conviction should make their voices heard in the public square. But they should do so as *one* moral voice, not *the* moral voice.

Q: How do you think church/state issues are going to be resolved?

A: Church/state separation and freedom of religion is a long and winding road we travel together in this nation. Every generation has its own challenges over how to work this fragile but crucial balance. In a recent *New York Times Magazine* article, Noah Feldman states that conservatives on the Right and secularists on the Left have both crossed the line on healthy church/state separation. Those on the Right want the state to endorse and support financially their moral positions. Those on the Left don't want *any* religious expression in the public square. He calls those on the Right "values evangelicals" and those on the Left "legal secularists." What he proposes is that "legal secularists" give up their demand that the public square be devoid of religious symbolism and moral advocacy and that "values evangelicals" give up their goal that the government "fund" their values and moral projects.[6]

I think Roger Williams would agree. Religious convictions have, correctly so, shaped our national character and our national laws, but our values have been freely debated and freely adopted, for, as Roger Williams believed, coercion of conscience is the greatest tyranny of all.

Q: Is this the end of the sermon?

A: Yes.

Q: Are you through?

A: For now.

CHAPTER NINETEEN

WELCOME ONE ANOTHER

Pseudo-community and Real Community in Christ

> *Every attempt at faith community is a necessary partici-*
> *pation in the eternal longing of God that we might be*
> *one . . . Growth does not just happen without the proper*
> *conditions. Two of those proper and necessary conditions*
> *are time and wisdom.*
> —Richard Rohr, *"All of Life Together Is a Stage"* in
> Sojourners

Hear, hear, all ye liberals and conservatives! All ye Republicans and Democrats, all ye boutique multicultur-alists and militant uniculturalists, all ye Left and Right, red and blue, this sermon is for you!

Romans 14 and 15 are important words for a divided church in America and for a divided America. Whether we call it culture war or values war or conservative versus liberal, our redness and blueness is killing us.

*This sermon, based on Romans 14 and 15, considers how Paul dealt with deep conflict in the first-century church in Rome and applies it to the cultural divide today in America and in the American church.

I begin with a *mea culpa*, which is Latin for "oops" or "my wrong," or to use today's vernacular, "my bad." (I think I'll stick to the Latin.)

In a sermon on end-of-life issues, I made a rather sweeping negative judgment on the Religious Right and political Right in their use of the term "culture of life." A couple came out of the service and said they loved the sermon and agreed with most of it, but they believed I had put the Religious Right in a box. They belong to the Religious Right, and by my dismissive comments about the Religious Right, they had felt dismissed.

I was wrong. We get in trouble when we think the Religious Right or the Religious Left is a monolithic uniform block of people. It is my hope, as senior minister, to help us be a community where Left and Right can honor each other and talk across the great divide in our culture. My comments were at cross-purposes with that goal. So *mea culpa*.

God has given this congregation a rare gift by providing us a generous mix of leftward people and rightward people. Serious, honest, and mutually respectful conversation inside this place as we worship, pray, and serve together can be a gift of shalom to our fractured nation.

What Paul was facing in the Roman church was a church divided over cultural, ethnic, religious, and moral issues.

The two main parties were named the "weak-in-faith" and the "strong-in-faith."

The "weak-in-faith" were the conservatives and were, as you might suspect, given their name by their opponents, who named themselves the "strong-in-faith." The "weak-in-faith" probably took the name and made it a badge of honor: "I'm conservative and proud of it!" The "strong-in-faith" had their own measure of spiritual pride: "We're the enlightened ones, the grown-up ones, the ones who really understand the gospel."

The presenting issue was the Jewish dietary regulations—what to eat and drink—but the deeper issues had to do with what was morally clean and unclean and how to make moral decisions.

Are my moral decisions based on rules that say what is right and wrong in every situation, or are they based on principles that you apply situation by situation? Does the *community* determine what is right and wrong, or does the *individual* determine that in his or her own personal faith? The issues went deep and grew hot.

I heard of a Baptist church near Louisville that split up in the nineteenth century. A guest speaker asked the question: "If a marauder came to your door and asked where your children were hidden, would you tell a lie and protect them from death or tell the truth and expose them to death?" The congregation got in such an awful row over the issue that they split into two congregations: the Lying Baptists and the Truthful Baptists.

Paul saw the fissure in the Roman church between the "weak-in-faith" and the "strong-in-faith." The "weak-in-faith," the conservatives, said that they needed the law of God. They were not strong enough or smart enough to know what was right and wrong in every decision and do it; so they would continue to follow the law. The "strong-in-faith," the liberals, said that Christ had freed them from the law and that they, in their personal relationship with God, could determine the right and the wrong.

The big problem was not the difference itself, but that the groups did not like each other very much because of the difference and would just as soon not be in church with the other group.

So here is Paul's message to the groups. He himself was in the "strong-in-faith" camp, but he wanted a church that could include both. I will summarize and paraphrase chapter 14 but will substitute the word "conservatives" where the text says "weak-in-faith" and "liberals" where it says "strong-in-faith."

14:1	Let the liberals welcome the conservatives but not for quarrels over convictions.
14:3	Let the liberal not despise the conservative, and let the conservative not pass judgment on the liberal, for God has welcomed the liberal.

14:4	Who are you to pass judgment on the servant of another? Your brother/sister, whether liberal or conservative, is the *Lord's* servant, not yours. And the Lord helps both to stand.
14:5-9	One person's freedom is in honor of the Lord. Another person's strict obedience is in honor of the Lord. Let it be so for both. Whether we live or die, we are the Lord's.
14:10-12	Why do you conservatives pass judgment on the liberals? And why do you liberals despise the conservatives? All of us will stand before the judgment seat of Christ, and each of us will have to give an account for him or herself. (You'd think that would keep us occupied enough without our trying to keep everybody else's books!)
14:14	On behalf of the liberals Paul says, "Nothing in itself is unclean!" On behalf of the conservatives Paul says, "But if you think it is unclean, it is unclean!"
14:15-20	Against the conservatives Paul says: "Everything is clean." But against the liberals Paul adds, "Do not let your liberated style of life cause your brother or sister to stumble. If you flaunt your freedom and thereby injure another or wound the conscience of another, you are not walking in love."
	To the conservative he says, "You must not coerce the conscience of another." To the liberal he says, "You must not undermine the conscience of another."
	To both groups he says, "Do not make your issues more important than the 'work of God.' Follow after the things that make for peace and build up and edify one another."
14:23	To both he says, "Whatever does not proceed from faith is sin." That is, as best as I can understand this phrase, you must live your life out of your personal, faithful relationship with Christ. Do not let your

conservative or liberal brother or sister intrude upon that faith relationship. Do not let them stand between you and your God. If you act apart from your faith relationship to Christ, that is sin.

14:23   There was a third group in the church, those Paul called "the doubters," the waverers, the ones caught in the middle, the confused moderates. They are caught in the crossfire between Right and Left. Paul says to them: you belong to Christ, not to the Left or to the Right. Determine in your heart of hearts, in relation to Christ, how you are to live. Act from the inside out, not from the pressure of any group.

14:17   Paul sums up with this statement (a little out of order): "For the kingdom of God is not food and drinking [not liberal or conservative] but righteousness and peace and joy in the Holy Spirit."

That's where the kingdom is, in these three. Righteousness: what the Bible calls holiness, right living, right relation. Peace: well-being, wholeness, unity. And joy. If there is no joy, there is no God. Holiness, wholeness, happiness. When three are happening, the kingdom is happening. If most of what you are doing is quarreling over convictions, that's not the kingdom. Paul does not want either side conquering or converting the other. His goal is the *peace of Christ manifest in the unity of reconciled diversity.*

15:5-6   So in chapter 15 Paul says, "Bear with one another in your differences. Live in harmony that together you may with *one mouth* glorify the God and Father of our Lord Jesus Christ."

15:7   And then he says with the final imploring words: "Welcome one another, therefore, just as Christ has welcomed you, for the glory of God!"

From A to Z we can find issues to divide us:

a.   alcohol, abortion, Arminianism
b.   birth control, biblical infallibility, baptism
c.   conservation, Calvinism, corporate ethics
d.   divorce, denominational politics
e.   ecology, economics
f.   feminism, fundamentalism, faith healing
g.   geopolitics
h.   homosexuality, hymns we like or don't like
i.   Iraq, Islam
j.   Jesus' humanity and divinity, judicial appointees
k.   kingdom of God
l.   liberalism, liberation theology
m.   multiculturalism, moratorium on the death penalty
n.   nationalism, nuclear weapons, nuclear power
o.   original sin, opinionated people (those *other* opinionated people, of course)
p.   pacifism, papal infallibility, passing the peace
q.   quest for the historical Jesus
r.   red-stateness and blue-stateness
s.   spiritual gifts, sexuality, Shoemaker
t.   the Trinity, taxes
u.   universalism, the United Nations
v.   violence in human society
w.   George W., war, weapons of mass destruction, worship styles
x.   xenophobia (fear of one who is different), exclusion of the strangers, the immigrant
y.   Yankees and Red Sox, yellow-dog Democrats
z.   Zen Buddhism

Some of these issues are of great importance, and Christ may call you to get involved in them, but let us remember *Christ* is most important of all, and in him we have real community.

M. Scott Peck says that real community goes through stages: 1) Pseudo-community, where our unity is based on superficial alikeness and we don't really acknowledge our differences. 2) Chaos, when our differences collide and we become disoriented. 3) Emptiness, when we experience the death of pseudo-community and death of the illusions with which we live. 4) Finally, community, real community that comes as we learn to love each other as we really are.[1]

All communities and deep relationships and marriages go through these stages, then go through them again. Stanley Hauerwas has what I have heard him refer to as "Hauerwas's Law." It goes, "We always marry the wrong person. We never know whom we marry; we just think we do."[2] Then we discover who they really are. Then true marriage begins: Learning to love the person you *have*, not the one you imagined.

Conclusion

We think our issues are so important; then we discover that what is really important is each other, and the Christ who has brought us together.

Fred Craddock tells the story of a friend and his missionary family under house arrest in China. One day they were told they were free to leave and return to America. They had twenty-four hours to pack and could only take two hundred pounds with them.

The parents and the two children had lived in China for years. How could they decide what to bring? They took out scales and weighed and chose and chose and weighed again until they had exactly two hundred pounds. The typewriter, the vase, the essential clothes.... Two hundred pounds to the ounce.

When they met the soldier at the airport, "The soldier asked, 'Ready to go?'

'Yes.'

'Did you weigh everything?'

'Yes.'

'You weighed the kids?'

'No, we didn't.'

'Weigh the kids.'

And in a moment, typewriter and vase and all became trash." [3]

"Welcome one another," says Paul, cherish one another, treasure one another, "as Christ has welcomed you, for the glory of God" (Rom. 15:7).

How dear you are, how dear each of you. Behold one another; behold the Christ in each other.

POSTSCRIPT

Praying for the President

In September of 2004 in the midst of the heated presidential campaign, President Bush came to Charlotte for a fundraising event at the home of one of my congregation's members. The family called and asked if I would offer a prayer at the dinner. They knew I had spoken publicly of my reservations about some of President Bush's policies, but they still asked. What was I to do? In earlier days, and in less rancorous times, it might not have been a controversial thing to pray for a president. I had said in sermons that we should pray for the president in these difficult days and had led prayers in worship for him. Now I was asked to pray for him in his presence and in a highly politicized environment. Here is the prayer I prayed at dinner, September 17, 2004.

Holy One of all the earth, all nations, all peoples, we pause at this meal together to give you thanks. We thank you for daily food given to us in such rich measure in this land.

We are grateful for the remarkable Providence that gave birth to this nation, for its speechless beauty and lavish bounty and for the divine gift of freedom which this nation has established and protected and offered as a light to the nations.

We thank you, O God, for the strength of leadership in President Bush and pray for him in the enormous responsibilities he carries everyday for our welfare and the welfare of the world.

Give him your steadying hand, your guiding wisdom, and a deep well of strength.

And give to us a renewal of dedication to this nation that we might ever be a city on a hill, shining your light, a beacon of freedom, an exemplar of justice, compassion embodied, and your instrument for the healing of the nations.

In your holy name,

Amen.

NOTES

Preface

1. Paul Hanson, *The Dawn of Apocalyptic* (Philadelphia: Fortress Press, 1975), 11-12.
2. Kim Stafford, *Early Morning: Remembering My Father, William Stafford* (Saint Paul, Minn.: Graywolf Press, 2002), 63.
3. Richard A. Posner, "Bad News," *New York Times Book Review* (July 31, 2005), 9.

Introduction

1. Karen Armstrong, *The Battle for God: A History of Fundamentalism* (New York: Random House, 2001), xiii.
2. Hans Küng, *Theology for the Third Millennium: An Ecumenical View* (New York: Doubleday, 1988), 209.
3. John Neuhaus, *The Naked Public Square* (Grand Rapids, Mich.: William B. Eerdmans, 1984).
4. Stephen L. Carter, *The Culture of Disbelief* (New York: HarperCollins, 1993).
5. Rowan Williams, *Arius: Heresy and Tradition* (Grand Rapids, Mich.: William B. Eerdmans, 2001), 24-25.

Chapter 1: The Education of a Baptist Boy from the South

1. Carlyle Marney, oral tradition.
2. For more on this, see Daniel Berrigan, *The Trial of the Catonsville Nine* (Boston: Beacon Press, 1970).
3. Reinhold Niebuhr, *The Children of Light and the Children of Darkness* (New York: Charles Scribner's Sons, 1944), xi.
4. Kevin Phillips, *American Theocracy* (New York: Viking Press, 2006), 99-262.
5. Ralph C. Wood in *Flannery O'Connor and the Christ-Haunted South*

163

(Grand Rapids, Mich.: William B. Eerdmans Publishing Co., 2004) said O'Connor is "reputed to have altered the John 8:32 verse."

Chapter 2: America and Providence

1. John Winthrop quoted in *The American Puritans: Their Prose and Poetry,* ed. Perry Miller (Garden City, N.Y.: Doubleday, 1956), 83.
2. H. Richard Niebuhr, *The Kingdom of God in America* (New York: Harper Torchbook, 1959).
3. John Winthrop, "A Model of Christian Charity," in *The American Puritans: Their Prose and Poetry,* 83.
4. Reinhold Niebuhr and Alan Hermert, *A Nation So Conceived* (New York: Charles Scribner & Sons, 1963), 123.
5. R. W. B. Lewis, *The American Adam* (Chicago: University of Chicago Press, 1955).
6. Gerhard Sauter, "A City on a Hill," in *Loving God with Our Minds: The Pastor as Theologian,* ed. Michael Welker and Cynthia A. Jarvis (Grand Rapids, Mich.: William B. Eerdmans, 2004), 25.
7. Arthur M. Schlesinger Jr., *The Cycles of American History* (Boston: Houghton Mifflin Company, 1986), 19.
8. Ibid., 20-21.
9. Cited in Schlesinger, *The Cycles of American History,* 14.
10. Ibid.
11. Cited in Sauter, "A City on a Hill," 22.
12. From *Abraham Lincoln: Speeches and Writings 1859-1865* (The Library of America, 1984), 415. Lincoln's phrase "the last best, hope of earth" has often been heard as a triumphalist phrase. But read in context you sense the fragile conditionality of this hope. Moreover, often the comma is misplaced—"last, best hope of earth"—which communicates a more grandiose tint than Lincoln intended. I think the plainer, clearer meaning of the phrase is "the latest best hope of earth."
13. Ibid., 209.
14. Reinhold Niebuhr, *The World Crisis and American Responsibility* (New York: Association Press, 1958), 12.
15. *New York Times,* March 2002, editorial.
16. Niebuhr and Hermert, *A Nation So Conceived,* 126.
17. Reinhold Niebuhr, *The Irony of American History* (New York: Charles Scribner & Sons, 1952), 130.
18. Ibid., 156.
19. Ibid., 174.
20. Sauter, "A City on a Hill," 26. For Robert Bellah's development of his phrase "civil religion" see his *The Broken Covenant: American Civil Religion in a Time of Trial* (New York: Seabury Press, 1975).

21. The words are Gehard Sauter's in "A City on a Hill," 17.

22. Paul D. Hanson, *The People Called: The Growth of Community and the Bible* (Louisville: Westminster John Knox Press, 2001), 520.

Chapter 3: The Spiritual and Political Virtue of Reverence

1. "The Second Coming," *The Collected Works of W. B. Yeats, Vol. 1: The Poems, Revised,* ed. Richard J. Finneran (New York: McMillan Publishing Company, 1924).

2. Robert Woodruff, *Reverence: Renewing a Forgotten Virtue* (Oxford: Oxford University Press, 2001), 1-2.

3. Ibid., 8.

4. Ibid., 15.

5. Allen Guelzo, *Abraham Lincoln: Redeemer President* (Grand Rapids, Mich.: William B. Eerdmans, 1999).

6. See Guelzo, *Abraham Lincoln: Redeemer President,* 362.

7. Ibid., 463.

8. Ibid., 5.

9. Ibid., 326.

10. Ibid., 322.

11. Ibid., 341.

12. Ibid.

13. As cited by David Brooks in a *New York Times* column, May 5, 2005.

14. William Lee Miller, *Lincoln's Virtues: An Ethical Biography* (New York: Vintage Books, 2003), 286.

15. Cited in *Abraham Lincoln: Speeches and Writings 1859-1865* (New York: The Library of America, 1984), 209.

16. Ibid., 224.

17. Ibid., 536.

18. Cited in Guelzo, *Abraham Lincoln: Redeemer President,* 362.

19. *Abraham Lincoln: Speeches and Writings,* 686-87.

20. Guelzo in *Abraham Lincoln: Redeemer President,* 447, summarizes with these words: "But Lincoln's own peculiar providentialism, his Calvinized deism, in fact played a controlling role in the outcome of the Civil War. ... in the most specific instance, providence was what allowed him to overrule the moral limitations of liberalism. To do liberalism's greatest deed—the emancipation of the slaves—Lincoln had to step outside liberalism and surrender himself to the direction of an overruling divine providence whose conclusions he had by no means prejudged."

Chapter 4: The Promise of Post-Constantinian Christianity

1. John Howard Yoder, *The Royal Priesthood: Essays Ecclesiological and Ecumenical*, ed. Michael G. Corturight (Grand Rapids, Mich.: William B. Eerdmans Publishing Co., 1994), 194.
2. Ibid., 195.
3. Ibid., 194-97.
4. Ibid., 64.
5. Ibid., 208.
6. Ibid., 210.
7. Yoder's translation of Matthew 20:25-27 in his *Preface to Theology* (Grand Rapids, Mich.: Brazos Press, 2002), 245.
8. Yoder, *The Royal Priesthood*, 210.
9. Ibid., 212.
10. Ibid., 215.
11. Ibid., 217.

Chapter 5: Fundamentalism and Secularism Reconsidered in Our Post-9/11 World

1. Martin E. Marty and R. Scott Appleby, eds., *Fundamentalism Comprehended* (Chicago: University of Chicago Press, 1995), 3.
2. Karen Armstrong, *The Battle for God: A History of Fundamentalism* (New York: Random House, 2001), xiii.
3. Ibid., 370-71.
4. Bruce Lincoln, *Thinking about Religion after September 11* (Chicago: University of Chicago Press, 2003).
5. Ibid., 5.
6. G. K. Chesterton, in his observations of the pervasive religious character of American life and of its "creed," The Declaration of Independence and the Constitution.

Chapter 6: Public Church in America

1. Martin E. Marty, *The Public Church: Mainline—Evangelical—Catholic* (New York: Crossroad, 1981), 3. This book grew out of Marty's "Public Religion Project." You may observe its work on its website: http://marty-center.uchicago.edu/research/publicreligion.shtml
2. Martin E. Marty in his foreword to Parker Palmer, *The Company of*

Strangers: Christians and the Renewal of America's Public Life (New York: Crossroad, 1997), 13.

3. Marty, *The Public Church*, 17.

4. Amin Maalouf, *In the Name of Identity: Violence and the Need to Belong* (New York: Penguin Books, 2000). Its original title was *Identités meurtrières*, "murderous identities."

5. Marty, *The Public Church*, 8.

6. Benjamin Franklin, "Proposals Relating to the Education of Youth in Philadelphia" in *Benjamin Franklin: Selections*, ed. Chester E. Jorgensorz and Frank Luther Mott (New York: Hill and Wang, 1962), 203.

7. Will Campbell, *Up to Our Steeples in Politics* (New York: Paulist Press, 1979), 59.

8. Bill Moyers, "Welcome to Doomsday," *New York Review of Books*, vol. 52, no. 5 (March 24, 2005): 1 (web edition).

9. The Public Religion Project website: http://marty-center.uchicago.edu/research/publicreligion.shtml

10. All the quotations here are taken from the website of the Public Religion Project, "Public Religion in America Today," by Martin E. Marty and Edith L. Blumhofer.

Chapter 7: Praying with Jesus in an Age of "Sacred Violence"

1. Cited in Bruce Lincoln, *Holy Terrors: Thinking about Religion after September 11* (Chicago: University of Chicago Press, 2003).

2. For my reflection on all nine of Jesus' prayers recorded in the Gospels, see *Finding Jesus in His Prayers* (Nashville: Abingdon Press, 2004).

3. Frye Gaillard (pers. commun.) from interviews in preparation for his book, *Cradle of Freedom: Alabama and the Movement That Changed America* (Tuscaloosa, Ala.: University of Alabama Press, 2004).

4. This essay and his brother's essay taking the opposite position "Must We Do Nothing?" are found in *War and Crucifixion: Essays on Peace, Violence and "Just War"* (Chicago: The Christian Century Foundation, 2002).

5. Wendell Berry, *Citizenship Papers* (Washington, D.C.: Shoemaker and Hoard, 2003), 14.

6. Flannery O'Connor, *Mystery and Manners: Occasional Prose*, ed. Sally and Robert Fitzgerald (New York: Farrar, Straus and Giroux, 2000), 114.

Chapter 8: America's Place in the World

1. *National Security Strategy.* Available online at http://www.whitehouse.gov/nsc/nss/2006/

2. Wendell Berry, *Citizenship Papers* (Washington, D.C.: Shoemaker and Hoard, 2003).

3. Jack Perry, "Family of Nations or World Empire" (unpublished essay), October 26, 2002.

4. Quoted in the *Charlotte Observer*, October 11, 2002.

5. Jack Perry, "America's Place in the World" (unpublished essay), May 22, 2003.

6. Cited in Arthur M. Schlesinger, *The Cycles of American History* (Boston: Houghton Mifflin Company, 1986), 68.

7. Ibid., 14. Schlesinger cites Sacvan Bercovitch for the phrase "elect nation" in *The Puritan Origins of the American Self* (New Haven: Yale University, 1975) and E. L. Tuveson for the phrase "redeemer nation" in *Redeemer Nation: The Idea of America's Millennial Role* (Chicago: University of Chicago Press, 1968).

8. Paul Tillich, *Systematic Theology*, vol. 1 (Chicago: University of Chicago Press, 1967), 134. See also vol. 3, 102.

9. Cited in Berry, *Citizenship Papers*, 5.

Chapter 9: The Politics of Doomsday

1. Mark Juergensmeyer, *Terror in the Mind of God* (Berkeley: University of California Press, 2000), 6.

2. Kim Stafford, *Early Morning: Remembering My Father, William Stafford* (Saint Paul, Minn.: Graywolf Press, 2002), 141.

3. Bill Moyers, "Welcome to Doomsday," *New York Review of Books*, vol. 52, no. 5 (March 24, 2005): 3 (web edition).

4. Yehezkel Landau in Barbara Rossing, *The Rapture Exposed* (Boulder, Colo.: Westview Books, 2005), 13, 44.

5. Paul Hanson, *The Dawn of Apocalyptic* (Philadelphia: Fortress Press, 1975), 11-12.

6. Ibid., 11. "Prophetic eschatology we define as a religious perspective which focuses in prophetic announcement to the nation of the divine plan for Israel and the world which the prophet has witnessed unfolding in the divine council and which he translates into the terms of plain history, real politics and human instrumentality, that is, the prophet interprets for the king and the people how the plans of the divine council will be effected within the context of their nation's history and the history of the world."

7. Paul D. Hanson, "Old Testament Apocalyptic Reexamined," *Interpretation*, 25, (1971): 454-79. "In classical prophecy the realm of human history was the realm within which the covenant relationship between Yahweh and his people was being carried out; historical events were carriers of cosmic significance. They were not bound to an inevitable progression toward a predetermined end. The people could repent, Yahweh could change his mind, prophesied judgment could be transformed into salvation" (478).

8. Hanson, *The Dawn of Apocalyptic*, 11-12. "Apocalyptic eschatology we

define as a religious perspective which focuses on the disclosure (usually esoteric in nature) to the elect of the cosmic victory of Yahweh's sovereignty—especially as it relates to his acting to deliver his faithful—which disclosure the visionaries have largely ceased to translate into the terms of plain history, real politics and human instrumentality due to a pessimistic view of reality growing out of the bleak post-exile conditions within which those associated with the visionaries found themselves. The conditions seemed unsuitable to them as a context for the envisioned restoration of God's prophecy." See also Klaus Koch and his important work *The Rediscovery of Apocalyptic* (Napierville, Ill.: Alec R. Allenson, Inc., 1970), 28 ff.

9. Paul Hanson summarized the historical conditions which gave rise to the apocalyptic imagination in the period of Hebrew history: "All existing cultic and political structures would be removed by divine judgment, to be replaced by a new order characterized by the vindication of the faithful remnant of God's eternal reign of righteousness, peace and prosperity." *The People Called: The Growth of Community and the Bible* (Louisville: Westminster John Knox Press, 2001), 347.

10. Paul Hanson, *The Dawn of Apocalyptic*, 12. "Despite the difference in the form of prophetic and apocalyptic eschatology, it must be emphasized that the essential vision of restoration persists in both, the vision of Yahweh's people restored as a holy community in a glorified Zion." The word "millennialism" is often used to describe groups that believe in the imminent coming of Christ and the establishment of his "thousand year" reign on earth. N. T. Wright (*The Millennium Myth* [Louisville, Ky.: Westminster John Knox Press, 1999]) observes: "The millennial instinct, at its best, means simply this: The ineradicable belief that the creator of the world intends to rescue the world, not to abolish it. His plans are designed for earth, not just for heaven" (19). Millennial thinking has spurred liberals to social change, as in the nineteenth-century abolitionist movement. It has also led to extremist groups like the Branch Davidians. See Stephen L. Cook, *Prophecy and Apocalypticism* (Minneapolis: Fortress Press, 1995) for a study of millennialism and apocalyptic.

11. In *Showings*, chapter 13, trans. Edmund College, O.S.A. and James Walsh, S.J. (New York: Paulist Press, 1978), 149.

12. Karen Armstrong, *The Battle for God: A History of Fundamentalism* (New York: Random House, 2001), x. "Premillennialism was, therefore, fueling the resentment experienced by fundamentalists by allowing them to cultivate fantasies of revenge that were quite out of keeping with the spirit of Jesus."

13. Mark Juergensmeyer, *Terror in the Mind of God*, 10.

14. Mark Juergensmeyer, *Violence and the Sacred in the Modern World* (London: Frank Cass, 1992), 112, 114.

15. David Frum and Richard Perle, *An End to Evil: How to Win the War on Terror* (New York: Random House, 2003), 7.

Chapter 10: Conversing with Jesus in Time of War

1. Wendell Berry, *Jayber Crow* (Washington, D.C.: Counterpoint Press, 2000), 142.

2. George Santayana, *The Life of Reason* (Amherst, N.Y.: Prometheus Books, 1998), 180.

Chapter 11: "If You Being Evil"

1. Susan Neiman, *Evil in Modern Thought* (Princeton, N.J.: Princeton University Press, 2002), 275.
2. These two essays are collected in *War as Crucifixion: Essays on Peace, Violence and "Just War"* (Chicago: The Christian Century Foundation, 2002).
3. Ibid., 17-23.
4. Ibid., 24-29.

Chapter 12: The Death of Jesus, Which Is Life to the World

1. This phrase comes from the work of René Girard. Theological uses of his work are exemplified by James Alison, *Raising Abel,* and Gil Baillie, *Violence Unveiled.*
2. Flannery O'Connor, "A Good Man Is Hard to Find," *The Complete Stories* (New York: Farrar, Straus and Giroux, 1973), 131.
3. Paul Johnson, *A History of Christianity* (New York: MacMillan, 1976), 29.
4. Martin Luther King Jr., *Where Do We Go from Here, Chaos or Community?* (New York: Harper and Row Publishers, 1967), 62-63.
5. Martin Luther King Jr., *A Testament of Hope: The Essential Writings and Speeches of Martin Luther King, Jr.,* ed. James Melvin Washington (San Francisco: HarperSanFrancisco, 1986), 267.

Chapter 13: Ground Zero Spirituality

1. Robert Nathan, "Sonnet VI," in *The Questing Spirit: Religion in the Literature of Our Time,* ed. Halford E. Luccock (Whitefish, Mont.: Kessinger Publishing, 2005). Originally published as *A Winter Tide: Sonnets and Poems* (New York: Alfred E. Knopf, 1935).
2. Generally speaking, apocalyptic views on the end of the world put the "end" in God's hand because human hands have become too weak and human hearts too evil.
3. I am indebted to Susan Neiman for her reflections on the impact of the Lisbon earthquake on our ways of thinking in *Evil in Modern Thought* (Princeton, N.J.: Princeton University Press, 2002).
4. Ibid., 243.
5. Ibid., 49.

6. *700 Club*, September 13, 2001. [Official transcript not available from *700 Club*. Cited in Bruce Lincoln, *Holy Terrors: Thinking About Religion After September 11* (Chicago: University of Chicago Press, 2003), 106.]

Chapter 14: The Revelatory Crisis of Abu Ghraib Prison

1. Available online at http://www.whitehouse.gov/nsc/nss
2. Robert Fuller, "What Divides Americans," first published in *Newsday*, Long Island, N.Y., August, 3 2003.
3. Mark Bowden, "Lessons of Abu Ghraib," *Atlantic Monthly*, July/August 2004.
4. David Brooks, "For Iraqis to Win, the U.S. Must Lose," *New York Times*, May 11, 2004.
5. Reinhold Niebuhr, *The Irony of American History* (New York: Charles Scribner's Sons, 1952), viii.
6. Ibid., 146.
7. Ibid., 162.
8. Ibid., 156.
9. Ibid., 173 (emphasis mine).

Chapter 15: A Deeper Patriotism

1. Cited in David L. Holmes, *The Religion of the Founding Fathers* (Ann Arbor, Mich.: The Clements Library, University of Michigan, 2003), 65.
2. Ibid.
3. Ibid., 77.
4. Ibid., 81-82.
5. Ibid., 94.
6. Ibid., 96.
7. L. P. Harley, *The Go-Between* (London: H. Hamilton, 1953; New York: New York Review Books Classics; repr. 2002), 17.

Chapter 16: How to Be Christian in an Election Year

1. Stanley Hauerwas, *Performing the Faith: Bonhoeffer and the Practice of Nonviolence* (Grand Rapids, Mich.: Brazos Press, 2004), 15.
2. Quoted in William Sloane Coffin, *The Heart Is a Little to the Left: Essays on Public Morality* (Hanover, N.H.: University Press of New England, 1999), 9.

Chapter 17: The Church at Prayer at Election Time

1. Martin E. Marty, *The Public Church: Mainline—Evangelical—Catholic* (New York: Crossroad, 1981), 3. See also chapter 6.
2. Readings were from The Declaration of Independence and Lincoln's Second Inaugural Address. Scripture lessons included Deuteronomy 30:15-16; 2 Chronicles 7:4; Micah 6:6-8; Proverbs 14:34; Matthew 22:15-22.
3. Ed Williams, "Prayers for Our Nation," *Charlotte Observer*, November 3, 2004.
4. Henri Nouwen, *The Genesee Diary* (Garden City, N.Y.: Image Books, 1981), 134.
5. Rowan Williams, "Intercessory Prayers," in *Open to Judgement* (London: Darton, Longman and Todd, 1994), 139.

Chapter 18: County Commissioners, Roger Williams, and Us

1. Cited in Mary Lee Settle, *I, Roger Williams* (New York: W. W. Norton, 2001), 24.
2. Edwin S. Gaustad, *Roger Williams* (New York: Oxford University Press, 2005), 53.
3. Ibid., 40.
4. Cited in Mary Lee Settle, *I, Roger Williams*, 270.
5. Cited in James William McClendon, *Systematic Theology*, vol. 2, *Doctrine* (Nashville: Abingdon Press, 1994), 486-87.
6. Noah Feldman, "A Church-State Solution," *New York Times Magazine* (July 3, 2005), 32. See also his new book on the subject, *Divided by God: America's Church-State Problem and What We Should Do About It* (New York: Farrar, Straus & Giroux, 2005).

Chapter 19: Welcome One Another

1. M. Scott Peck, *The Different Drum: Community Making and Peace* (New York: Touchstone, 1988).
2. Stanley Hauerwas, *A Community of Character: Toward a Constructive Christian Social Ethic* (Notre Dame: University of Notre Dame Press, 1981), 172.
3. *Craddock Stories*, ed. Mike Graves and Richard F. Ward (St. Louis: Chalice Press, 2001), 22-23.